Writing to Communicate

2

Paragraphs and Essays

THIRD EDITION

Cynthia A. Boardman

Spring International Learning Center
University of Arkansas, Fayetteville

Jia Frydenberg

Distance Learning Center
University of California Irvine

PEARSON
Longman

Writing to Communicate 2: Paragraphs and Essays, Third Edition

Pearson Education, 10 Bank Street, White Plains, NY 10606

Staff credits: The people who made up the *Writing to Communicate 2: Paragraphs and Essays, Third Edition* team, representing editorial, production, design, and manufacturing, are Danielle Belfiore, Wendy Campbell, Ann France, Laura Le Dréan, Michael Mone, Edith Pullman, Paula Van Ells, and Dorothy E. Zemach.

Cover photo: Momatiuk-Eastcott/Corbis
Text art and composition: Carlisle Publishing Services
Text font: 11.5/13 Minion
Illustrations: Steve Schulman

Photo credits:
Page xv © Richard T. Nowitz/Corbis; **p. 1** Tatiana Morozova/Shutterstock; **p. 2** © Michael S. Yamashita/Corbis; **p. 17** NASA Images/Alamy; **p. 25** Henry Westheim Photography/Alamy; **p. 26** Associated Press; **p. 30** JJ/Getty Images; **p. 49** © Sunnyart/Dreamstime.com; **p. 50** (first) © Paul A. Souders/Corbis, (second) © Kevin Schafer/Corbis, (third) © Peter Adams/Corbis, (fourth) © Staffan Widstrand/Corbis, (fifth) Art Kowalsky/Alamy, (sixth) Image State/Alamy; **p. 51** (first) Vladimirs Koskins/Shutterstock, (second) Eric Isselée/Shutterstock, (third) Najin/Shutterstock, (fourth) Trout55/Shutterstock, (fifth) rickt/Shutterstock; **p. 66** © Bloomimage/Corbis; **p. 67** (first) Don Farrall/Getty Images, (second) © Comstock/Corbis, (third) Nicola Gavin/Shutterstock, (fourth) Neil Beckerman/Getty Images; **p. 71** © Corbis; **p. 78** © 2007 Bob Sacha/Bob Sacha Photography; **p. 89** cloki/Shutterstock; **p. 91** © Jim Reed/Corbis; **p. 99** © Peter Johnson/Corbis; **p. 115** Hu Xiao Fang/Shutterstock; **p. 116** Malcolm Case-Green/Alamy; **p. 119** © Con Tanasiuk/Design Pics/Corbis; **p. 120** (first) © Corbis, (second) © C. Devan/zefa/Corbis, (third) © Comstock/Corbis, (fourth) © Ned Frisk Photography/Corbis; **p. 129** Arthur Tilley/Getty Images; **p. 144** Image Source Black/Alamy; **p. 157** Chris Fredriksson/Alamy; **p. 158** (first) © Robert Landau/Corbis, (second) © Michael S. Yamashita/Corbis

Library of Congress Cataloging-in-Publication Data
Boardman, Cynthia A.
   Writing to communicate: paragraphs and essays/Cynthia A. Boardman & Jia Frydenberg.—3rd ed.
      p. cm.
"Volume 2."
ISBN 0-13-235116-1 (student book : alk. paper)—ISBN 0-13-235115-3 (answer key : alk. paper)

1. English language—Textbooks for foreign speakers. 2. English language—Paragraphs—Problems, exercises, etc. 3. English language—Rhetoric—Problems, exercises, etc. 4. Academic writing—Problems, exercises, etc. I. Frydenberg, Jia. II. Title.
   PE1128.B5938 2008
   808'.0427—dc22

                                                                                            2007017465

ISBN-10: 0-13-235116-1
ISBN-13: 978-0-13-235116-4

Printed in the United States of America
8 9 10—V004—13 12 11 10

PEARSON LONGMAN ON THE **WEB**

Pearsonlongman.com offers online resources for teachers and students. Access our Companion Websites, our online catalog, and our local offices around the world.

Visit us at **www.pearsonlongman.com**.

DEDICATION

For the Bode Boys

and

For Bryan

ACKNOWLEDGMENTS

We wish to acknowledge and thank the many colleagues and students we've had during our many years of teaching. As every teacher knows, collegial support and collaboration make teaching all that more creative, and insightful questions and comments from curious, willing students make teaching truly a joy and remind us of the important work we do: teaching people of various cultures to communicate with and appreciate each other.

We also wish to thank the reviewers for their insights and suggestions, many of which were incorporated into this book: **Meghan Ackley**, University of Texas, Austin, TX; **Kimberly Bayer-Olthoff**, Hunter College IELI, New York, NY; **Michael Climo**, Antelope Valley College, Lancaster, CA; **Sally Gearhart**, Santa Rosa Junior College, Santa Rosa, CA; **Kate Johnson**, Intensive English Institute, Union County College, Elizabeth, NJ; **Laura Shier**, Portland State University, Portland, OR; **Dina Paglia**, Hunter College IELI, New York, NY; **Laurette Poulos Simmons**, Howard Community College, Columbia, MD; **Joanna Vaughn**, Language Studies International, Berkeley, CA.

Finally, we are indebted to the people at Pearson Education for their efforts in this project—Laura Le Dréan, whose faith in our work kept us going, to Dorothy E. Zemach, whose tireless efforts made this book unified and coherent; and to all the people in between: Danielle Belfiore, Wendy Campbell, Ann France, Michael Mone, Edith Pullman, and Paula Van Ells. Many, many thanks!

Cynthia A. Boardman

Jia Frydenberg

CONTENTS

CHAPTER 6   THE INTRODUCTORY PARAGRAPH 76
Nature vs. Nurture

CHAPTER 7   THE CONCLUDING PARAGRAPH 87
The State of the Earth

CHAPTER 8   BODY PARAGRAPHS 97
The Water Around Us

TO THE TEACHER

Welcome to the third edition of *Writing to Communicate: Paragraphs and Essays*. We have been extremely pleased by the positive reaction to our book, and we have taken note of the many excellent teacher and student suggestions that have helped make this third edition an even more effective teaching tool.

What's New and What's the Same

Based on feedback from teachers and students who have used the book, we have introduced four new components to this third edition. First of all, each chapter now begins with a vocabulary development section. There are also new exercises in every chapter. Each chapter has been reorganized to include four major sections:

- Section   I: Vocabulary Builder
- Section II: Writing Focus
- Section III: Structure and Mechanics
- Section IV: Writing to Communicate

Finally, we have added a section after each major part of the textbook. Called "Bringing It All Together," this short section reviews the writing and grammatical focus of the chapters in that part of the book.

However, the features that have made the *Writing to Communicate* textbook such a lasting fixture among writing books have been retained. We have kept the emphasis on accessible models of writing in this edition, although you will notice that most of the models have been rewritten to bring in new topical areas and to update the content. Secondly, the charts of organizational structures that teachers tell us they find so useful are still there. The same is true of the Peer Help Worksheets at the end of each chapter. Finally, the original organization of the book into three main parts (I: Paragraphs, II: The Essay, and III: Rhetorical Patterns) remains the same in this third edition.

Writing to Communicate is now *Writing to Communicate 2: Paragraphs and Essays*, and it is the second book in a series of writing books for the academic student. The first book, *Writing to Communicate 1: Paragraphs,* covers the paragraph for students at the high elementary level. The third book in the series, *Writing to Communicate 3: Essays and Short Research Papers,* takes high intermediate to advanced students through the process of writing a documented paper.

How to Use This Book

Section 1 of each chapter, the **Vocabulary Builder**, draws students into the topic area of that chapter. The vocabulary in this section reappears in the models and the writing assignments in Section 4. We suggest that you use the Vocabulary Builder section for open-ended vocabulary discussions; the words are not intended to be memorized.

Section 2 of each chapter is the **Writing Focus** section, where students study the organization of the type of writing they will do in that lesson. In this section for Part III, you will find many charts and tables—or *graphic organizers*. Please feel free to copy these graphic organizers onto a transparency to use in your classroom for easy reference for the students. The purpose of the graphic organizers and the model paragraphs and essays in Section 2 is for your students to see how the components or "building blocks" of a piece of writing fit together and how they build upon each other to shape a cohesive whole. We recommend that you allow plenty of time for your students to analyze the models in Section 2 so that, over time, the organizational patterns become second nature to them.

Section 3 of each chapter is the **Structure and Mechanics** section, which emphasizes meaningful use of sentence connectors, such as transitions, coordinating conjunctions, subordinating conjunctions, and prepositions, and the vocabulary needed to build the organizational pattern of the writing exercises. The sentence connectors that are introduced in Section 3 will be very useful for your students because these are the "signposts" of good cohesive writing in English.

The final section of each chapter, **Writing to Communicate,** contains the writing assignments for the chapter as well as the Paragraph Checklist or Peer Help Worksheet. In many cases, this will be where your students have a chance to use the vocabulary they studied in Section 1 for their own writing.

The Chapters

Part I
Chapters 1 and 2 review the most important aspects of paragraph structure. Chapter 3 is entirely new and focuses on the steps in the process of producing good writing. This chapter will be referred to in many of the subsequent chapters.

Part II
Each of the five chapters in this section focuses on one single aspect of the building blocks that make up an essay: the complete organization of an essay, the thesis statement, the introduction, the supporting paragraphs, and the conclusion of the essay.

Part III
This part contains four chapters. Each introduces a different essay pattern to meet different purposes of academic writing. This edition of the textbook has the following rhetorical patterns: process, classification, persuasion, and comparison/contrast.

Audience

The book is intended to fit into the middle level of a writing program that guides students from beginning to advanced writing in academic English at the college level. We expect that students who use this book have had some previous experience with writing paragraph-length compositions, as well as some exposure to the rhetorical structure of paragraphs. These students usually score in the 40–60 range on the Internet-based TOEFL® (IBT) or 433–497 on the paper-based TOEFL test. However, we have also had experience with students who score above this range who have benefited from the materials in this book.

Appendices

Many teachers want to use extra copies of three of the charts in the appendices to attach to students' work: General Peer Help Worksheet, Paragraph and Essay Evaluation, and Suggested Correction Symbols. These pages may be photocopied and distributed for classroom use.

Answer Key

An Answer Key with suggested answers to the exercises is published in a separate booklet.

TO THE STUDENT

This book is designed to help you become a better writer of American English. It will teach you about the process of writing. This process consists of more than just picking up a pencil and writing a paragraph or an essay from beginning to end. Writing is a process because it goes through many stages. It starts with understanding what is expected of you in a writing assignment. Next, it involves thinking about what you are going to write and planning how you are going to organize it. The final steps involve writing, checking your work, and rewriting. Being a good writer means you continually change, add to, and improve what you have already written.

The major focus of this book is the organization of academic essays; that is, essays that are written in college or university classes. These essays are somewhat formal in nature and, as you will find, very direct. This style of organization may or may not be the kind that you use in other languages or circumstances.

In addition to organization, you will learn other aspects of writing conventions, including punctuation, the use of connectors, and paragraph and essay format. To become a better writer, you must start with the basics of format and organization. Once these basics are under control (a process that may take some time), there is room for variation, as you will learn in later chapters.

Sometimes the hardest part of writing is deciding what you are going to say. That is why the models in this book are organized around topics familiar to most people. While you are doing the prewriting activities and reading the models, you should think about the topic and how it relates to you and your life. Then, when it's time to write, you will have some ideas about what you want to say.

Finally, most of what you learn from this book is applicable to other types of writing in English, such as business writing. By taking the time to learn the basics in this book, you will improve your overall ability to communicate in English. We hope that your experience with *Writing to Communicate 2* is both a valuable and an interesting one.

INTRODUCTION: WRITING IN ENGLISH

Writing to communicate dates back thousands of years. Writing started as symbols on a cave wall, and then, about 3,500 years ago, people began to use alphabets.

Different languages use different writing systems.

Different languages also use different writing styles of organization. **English** organization, for example, is fairly simple. English uses a straight line from beginning to end. For instance, when English speakers read an article, they expect the article to have a beginning, a middle, and an end. The beginning should say what the article is going to be about, the middle should talk about the topic of the article, and the end should say what the article was about. Here is a diagram of the English style of writing.[1]

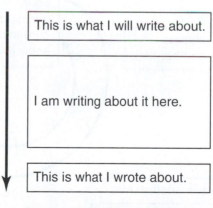

> This is what I will write about.
>
> I am writing about it here.
>
> This is what I wrote about.

Diagram 1: English Organization

Other languages organize writing differently. For example, **Spanish** organization is similar to English, but the line from beginning to end isn't so straight. Spanish speakers write about the topic, but here and there they add something that is not directly related to the topic. To a Spanish speaker, this makes the writing more interesting.

---

[1] *Source*: Based on Kaplan, R.B. "Cultural thought patterns in intercultural education." *Language Learning*, 16 (1), 1966.

Here is a diagram of the Spanish style of writing.

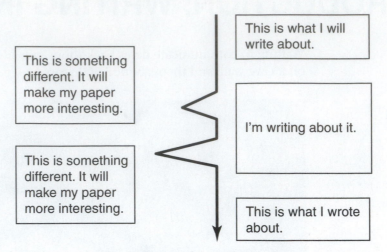

Diagram 2: Spanish Organization

The **Japanese** style of writing is often circular. This means that the topic comes at the end of the article. In fact, sometimes, the writer doesn't say what the topic is. Instead, the writer gives hints to help the reader guess the topic. Here is a diagram of the Japanese style of writing.

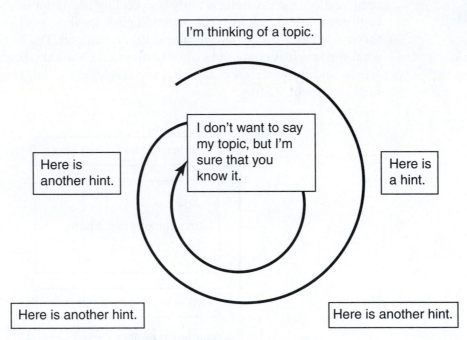

Diagram 3: Japanese Organization

Still another style of writing is used in Arabic. To be a good writer in Arabic, you need to write in a parallel style. This means that you write using coordinating conjunctions, such as *and*, *or*, or *but*. (You will learn more about these in Chapter 1.) English, on the other hand, uses more subordinating conjunctions, such as *when*, *before*, or *until*. (You will learn more about these in Chapter 3.) Arabic writing is also more repetitive than English writing, with the main points being restated in different ways throughout the text. To an Arabic reader, this style is elegant and what is expected, but it is not the style for academic English writing. Look at this diagram. It shows the repetition and coordination that is necessary for good Arabic writing.

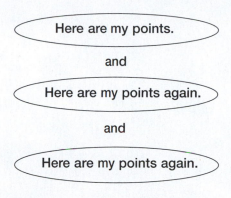

Diagram 4: Arabic Organization

It's important to understand that one style of writing isn't better than another, just as one language isn't better than another. The styles are just different. To be a successful writer in any language, you need to learn the writing style in addition to words and grammar rules.

In this book, you will learn the **American English** style of writing.

THE PARAGRAPH

THE ORGANIZATION OF PARAGRAPHS

Holidays Around the World

I VOCABULARY BUILDER

The words *holiday* and *vacation* have different meanings in the United States. A holiday is usually just one day, and it is celebrated by everyone on the same day. Some holidays are national holidays. These holidays are work-free days for most employees. Examples of these days are New Year's Day, Memorial Day, and Thanksgiving. Other holidays aren't work-free days, but people celebrate them anyway. Examples of these are Valentine's Day and Halloween. Vacations, on the other hand, are work-free periods for individuals at a time of their choosing. These people don't have to work, but everyone else does.

Read the list of activities that people typically do on holidays or vacations. Check (✔) the ones that you also do. Then share your answers with a partner or small group. Tell when you do the activities that you checked.

_____ Bring treats to your coworkers	_____ Remember a historical event	_____ Stay up until midnight
_____ Cook special foods	_____ Remember someone who died	_____ Take a trip
_____ Have a party	_____ Send holiday cards	_____ Watch a parade
_____ Have a picnic	_____ Stay home and watch TV	_____ Watch fireworks
_____ Listen to a speech		_____ Wear a costume

Basic Organization

The paragraph is the basic unit of academic writing in English. Students who want to study in a college or university need to learn how to write a paragraph because all other types of academic writing, such as essays, reports, compositions, and research papers, are based on the paragraph. In this chapter, you will learn about the organization of a paragraph.

Academic paragraphs have a very specific organizational pattern. When you follow this pattern, your paragraph will be easy for your reader to understand.

Look at this model paragraph. What is the purpose of each shaded part?

Model Paragraph 1

Golden Week

Golden Week in Japan is a combined celebration of four holidays.

The first takes place on April 29th, the birthday of the Emperor Showa, and commemorates[1] the 64 years that he was in power. It is a time for the Japanese people to remember this important period in their history. The second holiday in Golden Week is Constitutional Memorial Day. This day marks the establishment of the Japanese Constitution on May 3, 1947. The next holiday, on May 4th, is called Midorino-hi and is a day for people to be outside enjoying the environment. In fact, Midorino-hi means "green day." Children's Day, the fourth holiday of Golden Week, is on May 5th. This holiday celebrates the health and happiness of children. Traditionally, this day was Boys' Day, and some families still recognize this. For example, they fly flags shaped like carp[2] outside their homes to bring strength and success to their boys. In short, Golden Week is a whole week of celebration for the Japanese people.

[1]**commemorate** *v.* remember someone or something with a special action

[2]**carp** *n.* type of freshwater fish

What about you?

What's your favorite holiday? Why? Share your answer with a classmate.

This paragraph begins with a sentence that introduces the topic and main idea of the paragraph. It is called the **topic sentence**. The middle part of the paragraph is called the body, and it consists of sentences that explain, or support, the topic sentence. These sentences are called **supporting sentences**. The last sentence is called the **concluding sentence**, which ends the paragraph by reminding the reader of the main point of the paragraph.

Basic academic writing in English is linear in structure; that is, it has a beginning, a middle, and an end, and it continues directly from one part to the next. Once you have mastered this organizational pattern, you will be able to use it in almost all types of writing in English.

The Topic Sentence

A topic sentence is the most important sentence in a paragraph because it contains the main idea of the paragraph. A good topic sentence has two parts: the **topic** and the **controlling idea**. The topic is the subject of your paragraph. The controlling idea limits the topic of your paragraph. It shows the aspect of that topic that you want to explore in your paragraph. Look at these topic sentences:

➤ (New York) **is a fun place to be on New Year's Eve.**
     topic   controlling idea

➤ (New York) **has great entertainment.**
     topic   controlling idea

➤ (New York) **is the world's loudest city.**
     topic   controlling idea

Each of these topic sentences has the same topic, *New York*, but a different controlling idea. Each one would introduce a paragraph with different ideas and information.

Most academic writing is done to persuade the reader that a point of view is reasonable. For this reason, another important part of writing topic sentences is to write a sentence that has a clear point of view, which is usually the writer's opinion. A statement of fact is not an effective topic sentence because there is nothing more that can be said about it, and as a result, nothing to write in your paragraph. Look at these two sentences:

➤ Twenty-five people attended the company's Halloween party.

➤ The company's Halloween party was a bore, as usual.

The first sentence above is not an effective topic sentence because it is a fact. It is difficult to write more about this because it is either true or false. However, since the second sentence is an opinion, there is a lot the writer could say to convince the reader that the party was a bore. Therefore, it is an acceptable topic sentence.

Another common way to write a topic sentence is to divide a topic into different parts. Look at this sentence:

➤ (Ramadan) **has three important days within the month of fasting.**
     topic   controlling idea

For the topic sentence above, the writer explains the division of the topic into parts. That explanation is the controlling idea. Circle the topics and underline the controlling ideas in the sentences below.

➤ There are three main kinds of holidays.

➤ Planning a good Fourth of July party requires five specific steps.

■ PRACTICE 1: Identifying Topics and Controlling Ideas

Read each sentence. Circle the topic and underline the controlling idea.

1. India celebrates Christian, Hindu, and Islamic holidays.
2. It's fun to carve a Halloween pumpkin.
3. Independence Day is an important holiday in any country.
4. Going to big holiday parties is like a punishment to me.
5. Different countries have unique ideas about Santa Claus.
6. The Western world should have a holiday to recognize senior citizens.
7. It's important to honor your mother on Mother's Day.
8. Rain can ruin a picnic.

■ PRACTICE 2: Evaluating Topic Sentences

Read each sentence and decide if it is a good topic sentence. Remember that topic sentences should state an opinion or divide the topic into parts. If the sentence is a good topic sentence, circle the topic and underline the controlling idea. If the sentence is not a good topic sentence, cross it out.

1. Japan has three holidays that honor family members.
2. President Lincoln established Thanksgiving as the fourth Thursday in November.
3. Making a costume for Halloween takes a lot of hard work.
4. International Women's Day is March 8.
5. International Women's Day is an important day.
6. You need four days to plan a holiday party.
7. Africans celebrate Africa Day, which marks the end of colonial rule.
8. Different African nations celebrate Africa Day with different activities.
9. In some countries, May Day is also called Labor Day.
10. There are many reasons to stay home on New Year's Eve.

■ PRACTICE 3: Writing Topic Sentences

Choose two holidays that are celebrated in your country. Write a topic sentence for each holiday following this example.

Topic (holiday):   *Earth Day*

Controlling idea (what to   *How it is celebrated*
say about the holiday):

Topic sentence: *To celebrate Earth Day, my town organizes fun but useful activities.*

1. Topic: _____

   Controlling idea: _____

   Topic sentence: _____

   _____

(continued)

2. Topic: _____

   Controlling idea: _____

   Topic sentence: _____
   _____

The Body (Supporting Sentences)

Supporting sentences explain the topic sentence. One common way to do this is with facts. Look back at the model paragraph on page 3 and note the sentences with facts, such as:

> ➤ The second holiday in Golden Week is Constitutional Memorial Day.

> ➤ This day marks the establishment of the Japanese Constitution on May 3, 1947.

■ PRACTICE 4: **Analyzing Model Paragraph 2**

Answer these questions about the model paragraph below.

1. In the topic sentence, circle the topic and underline the controlling idea.
2. How many facts are given as support?

Model Paragraph 2

An Expensive Holiday

Valentine's Day is a very expensive holiday. Typically, people who are in love with each other exchange gifts. The gifts often cost a lot of money, sometimes as much as $100. If you don't spend that much, your sweetheart might think you don't care. For example, one of the most popular gifts is chocolate. One box of nice chocolates may cost $20 or more, which adds up to a million dollars or more spent in the United States on chocolate for a single day! Flowers are also a common gift, and they cost more than chocolate, so sales of flowers may amount to $5 million in one day! In addition, it is often expected that you and your sweetheart will go out to dinner on that evening. A romantic dinner at a nice restaurant may cost $100 or more per person. In conclusion, if you plan to celebrate Valentine's Day, make sure you have a lot of money.

A second way to support a topic sentence is with examples. In the model paragraph on page 3, the following supporting sentence is an example.

> ➤ For example, they fly flags shaped like carp outside their homes to bring strength and success to their boys.

■ PRACTICE 5: **Analyzing Model Paragraph 3**

Answer these questions about the model paragraph that follows.

1. In the topic sentence, circle the topic and underline the controlling idea.
2. How many examples are given as support?

Valentine's Day Overload[1]

Cupid

Three or four weeks before Valentine's Day, you begin to see an overabundance[2] of reminders of this only-for-lovers holiday almost everywhere. For example, you see red hearts and cupids in every shop and restaurant. Shops want you to buy a gift for your valentine, and restaurants hope that you will treat your valentine to an expensive dinner. Another example of Valentine's Day reminders is seeing the commercials on TV, which tell you about all the wonderful presents and cards that you can buy for that special someone. Even on your own computer, you find pop-up advertisements telling you where to get a gift for your valentine. Internet spam even tells you how to find a valentine if you don't have one. In short, it's completely impossible to hide from Valentine's Day, so, to keep your sanity, sit down and wait it out.

[1]**overload** *n.* too many things happening at the same time   [2]**overabundance** *n.* too many or too much

The third common way of supporting a topic sentence is by using an illustration that is based on a personal experience. This next model paragraph relates a personal experience about Valentine's Day.

■ PRACTICE 6: Analyzing Model Paragraph 4

Answer these questions about the model paragraph below.

1. In the topic sentence, circle the topic and underline the controlling idea.
2. How does the body of this paragraph support the topic sentence?

Model Paragraph 4

A Sad Valentine

Valentine's Day makes me feel bad if I am alone. For example, last Valentine's Day, I was alone because I had broken up with my boyfriend the week before. Instead of celebrating like I did the year before, I stayed in and ate a frozen pizza and a candy bar in front of the TV. I was so upset. Then I found the present that I was going to give him on Valentine's Day. It was a cute teddy bear[1] holding a big heart that said, "I love you!" As I held it, I realized that the only Valentine card I had received was from my grandmother. I started to cry. In conclusion, Valentine's Day can only be a happy day for me if I have someone to share it with.

[1] **teddy bear** *n.* a soft toy shaped like a bear

Major and Minor Supporting Sentences

In terms of organization, especially of expository paragraphs, there are two types of supporting sentences: **major supporting sentences** and **minor supporting sentences**. Major supporting sentences tell us about the topic sentence. Minor supporting sentences tell us more about the major supporting sentences.

■ PRACTICE 7: **Analyzing Supporting Sentences**

Look again at the paragraph "Golden Week" on page 3. Below, it has been diagrammed to show the parts of a paragraph, including the major and minor supporting sentences. Draw arrows to show that the major supporting sentences support the topic sentence and that the minor supporting sentences support the major supporting sentence above them. The first two have been done for you.

<u>Topic Sentence (TS)</u>

➤ Golden Week in Japan is a combined celebration of four holidays.

<u>Major Supporting Sentence (SS)</u>

➤ The first takes place on April 29th, the birthday of the Emperor Showa, and commemorates the 64 years that he was in power.

<u>Minor Supporting Sentence (ss)</u>

➤ It is a time for the Japanese people to remember this important period in their history.

<u>Major Supporting Sentence (SS)</u>

➤ The second holiday in Golden Week is Constitutional Memorial Day.

<u>Minor Supporting Sentence (ss)</u>

➤ This day marks the establishment of the Japanese Constitution on May 3, 1947.

<u>Major Supporting Sentence (SS)</u>

➤ The next holiday, on May 4th, is called Midorino-hi and is a day for people to be outside enjoying the environment.

<u>Minor Supporting Sentence (ss)</u>

➤ In fact, Midorino-hi means "green day."

<u>Major Supporting Sentence (SS)</u>

➤ Children's Day, the fourth holiday of Golden Week, is on May 5th.

<u>Minor Supporting Sentence (ss)</u>

➤ This holiday celebrates the health and happiness of children.

<u>Minor Supporting Sentence (ss)</u>

➤ Traditionally, this day was Boys' Day, and some families still recognize this.

<u>Minor Supporting Sentence (ss)</u>

➤ For example, they fly flags shaped like carp outside their homes to bring strength and success to their boys.

<u>Concluding Sentence (CS)</u>

➤ In short, Golden Week is a whole week of celebration for the Japanese people.

All major supporting sentences do *not* need to have the same number of minor supporting sentences. In fact, sometimes you will not have any minor supporting sentences at all.

■ **PRACTICE 8:** Diagramming a Paragraph

Diagram the paragraph "Valentine's Day Overload" on page 7 on a separate sheet of paper. Indicate the major supporting sentences and the minor supporting sentences. Use the example on page 8 as a guide.

The Concluding Sentence

The concluding sentence of a paragraph is generally needed in a stand-alone paragraph. Usually, a concluding sentence is a restatement of the topic sentence. That is, it gives the same information as the topic sentence, but the information is expressed in a different way. Concluding sentences usually start with a transition, such as *all in all, in conclusion, in short,* or *in summary.* Not all concluding sentences need a transition, however. You as the writer decide if it is necessary.

Look at this paragraph and underline the topic sentence and the concluding sentence. What synonym in the concluding sentence is the restatement for the controlling idea "not sad" in the topic sentence?

Model Paragraph 5

The Day of the Dead

Día de los Muertos, or Day of the Dead, is not a sad occasion in Mexico. In fact, it is a time of celebrating the continuity of life since death is a part of life. On Día de los Muertos, Mexicans usually go to the cemetery[1] where their ancestors and loved ones are buried. They bring bright and colorful flowers to decorate the graves[2] and honor their ancestors. Another way of remembering loved ones is to tell long stories about their lives. These stories can be funny and sad at the same time. There are also grand picnics at the cemeteries, where all kinds of delicious foods are served. The dessert is often sugar candy in the shape of a skull[3] or a skeleton.[4] In short, contrary to its name, Día de los Muertos is a happy, family-oriented holiday in Mexico.

[1]**cemetery** *n.* an area of land where dead people are buried
[2]**grave** *n.* a place where one dead person is buried
[3]**skull** *n.* the bones in the head
[4]**skeleton** *n.* the bones of the body

A second, less common way to conclude a paragraph is to write a sentence that summarizes the main points in the body of the paragraph.

As you read this paragraph, underline the major supporting sentences. Then notice how the concluding sentence mentions the topic of each major supporting sentence.

Model Paragraph 6

Celebrating the New Year

The new year is celebrated throughout the world at many different times, based on the solar[1] or lunar[2] calendar. January 1 is recognized throughout the world as the beginning of the new year, but this date is the beginning of the Christian year based on the Gregorian solar calendar. The Jewish new year is called Rosh Hashanah. It is celebrated in September or October because the Hebrew calendar is lunar. The Chinese new year, celebrated in many Asian countries, follows a lunar calendar and comes on a day between January 10 and February 19. Islamic countries also use a lunar calendar. Their new year celebration is in the spring, and the date varies depending on the year. In short, Christians use the solar calendar, whereas Jews, Asians, and Muslims use a lunar calendar to determine when to celebrate the new year.

[1]**solar** *adj.* related to the sun   [2]**lunar** *adj.* related to the moon

■ **PRACTICE 9: Choosing a Concluding Sentence**

Read the following paragraph. Choose the concluding sentence that you think is best by checking (✔) the box next to it. Then explain your choice to a classmate.

Sankt Hans

The Scandinavian holiday of Sankt Hans is a combination of a traditional popular celebration and a religious one. The old tradition was to celebrate the longest day of the year, June 21, as a magical time. In honor of the sun, people would light huge bonfires[1] and dance and sing. The old customs also included lots of good food cooked over smaller bonfires and plenty of homemade beer. When the Christian religion was introduced to Scandinavia about 1000 years ago, the religious authorities were not particularly pleased with these popular  pagan[2] rituals,[3] and they decided to dedicate the day to Saint Johannes instead. In fact, the name Sankt Hans is a simplification of Saint Johannes. Over time, however, most people have forgotten the religious meaning of Sankt Hans, and they have gone back to the traditional celebration with bonfires, music, food, and parties with family and friends.

---

[1]bonfire *n.* large piles of wood set on fire
[2]pagan *adj.* relating to a religion that is not one of the major religions of the world

[3]ritual *n.* traditional activities

❑ In short, Sankt Hans is an interesting Scandinavian holiday.

❑ In short, Scandinavians still celebrate Sankt Hans as they did over a thousand years ago.

❑ In short, both tradition and religion played a role in developing the current-day Scandinavian holiday Sankt Hans.

III STRUCTURE AND MECHANICS

Sentences and Punctuation

The use of punctuation marks varies greatly from language to language. In academic writing in English, the rules of punctuation must be followed carefully. To use punctuation marks correctly, you must have a basic understanding of sentence structure. A sentence must have an **independent clause**. Look at the meanings of these words to help you understand what an independent clause is.

independent: able to stand alone; not dependent on something else

clause: a group of words containing a subject and a verb

independent clause: a group of words that contains a subject and a verb and that can stand alone

Note that the basic punctuation pattern for a sentence is to begin it with a capital letter and end it with a period.

Sentence (an independent clause)

➤ **St. Patrick's Day honors** Irish Americans.
　　subject　　　　　　　verb

Not a sentence (not an independent clause)

➤ When Irish Americans are honored on St. Patrick's Day.

This is not independent because we don't know what happens when Irish Americans are honored.

Corrected Sentence:

➤ Restaurants serve green drinks when Irish Americans are honored on St. Patrick's Day.

Not a sentence (a phrase)

➤ Honoring Irish Americans on St. Patrick's Day.

This is not independent because there is no verb.

Corrected Sentence:

➤ Honoring Irish Americans on St. Patrick's Day is a long-held tradition.

■ **PRACTICE 10:** Identifying Sentences

Read each group of words and decide whether it is a sentence. If it is, put a capital letter at the beginning and a period at the end. If it isn't, work with a partner and change it into a complete sentence.

1. in the United States, religious holidays often become nonreligious
2. the government of the United States recognizes eight holidays by giving its employees the day off
3. parents hiding several hundred Easter eggs
4. when we spent a long holiday weekend in the mountains
5. most people look forward to long holiday weekends
6. after the celebration was over
7. lighting bonfires on the beach during the summer
8. in Germany, you bring a picnic to work on your birthday

Connecting Sentences

Using Coordinating Conjunctions

You can improve your writing by connecting two independent clauses into one sentence. This makes your writing more sophisticated and cohesive. One way to combine two sentences is to use a comma and a **coordinating conjunction**.

When coordinating conjunctions are used to combine two independent clauses, they establish a relationship between the sentences. The relationship depends on the coordinating conjunction that you choose. There are seven coordinating conjunctions, and you can easily remember them by remembering the word *FANBOYS*.

F	*for*	(cause)	Monday is a holiday, **for** it is Labor Day.
A	*and*	(addition)	Monday is a holiday, **and** Tuesday is a holiday.
N	*nor*	(choice)	Monday isn't a holiday, **nor** is Tuesday a holiday. (*Note:* When you use *nor* in this way, you must use question word order after it.)
B	*but*	(difference)	Monday is a holiday, **but** Tuesday is not a holiday.
O	*or*	(choice)	We'll celebrate the holiday on Monday, **or** we'll celebrate it on Tuesday.
Y	*yet*	(difference)	Monday is a holiday, **yet** Tuesday isn't a holiday.
S	*so*	(result)	Monday is a holiday, **so** we don't have to go to school.

Using Commas with Coordinating Conjunctions

There are three rules for using commas with coordinating conjunctions:

1. When coordinating conjunctions are used to connect independent clauses, they are preceded by a comma.

   ➤ April Fool's Day was my favorite holiday as a child, **and** it is still fun for me as an adult.

   ➤ Martin Luther King Day is a national holiday, **yet** some employees must work.

   ➤ Arbor Day honors trees, **so** many people plant trees on this day.

   ➤ We can't go out to celebrate, **nor** can we stay home.

2. If the clause that comes after the coordinating conjunction doesn't have a subject and verb, do not use a comma.

   ➤ Annie got up late **and** forgot to call her mother on Mother's Day.

3. Although you may see coordinating conjunctions begin a sentence after a period, this is not considered good academic style. Instead, begin a new sentence with a transition with the same meaning. (Chapter 4 discusses transitions.)

Nonacademic style

   ➤ We were going to go to the Halloween party. **But** we didn't know what time it started.

Academic style

   ➤ We were going to go to the Halloween party. **However**, we didn't know what time it started.

■ **PRACTICE 11: Combining Sentences with Coordinating Conjunctions**

Combine the pairs of sentences with an appropriate coordinating conjunction. Be sure to use a comma between the sentences. Try to use each coordinating conjunction. More than one correct answer is possible. The first one has been done for you.

1. Bastille Day commemorates the birth of the modern nation of France. The French celebrate it with parades and parties.

   Bastille Day commemorates the birth of the modern nation of France, so the French celebrate it with parades and parties.

   OR

   The French celebrate Bastille Day with parades and parties, for it commemorates the birth of the modern nation of France.

2. Min Soo hates shopping for the winter holidays. He does all his shopping in the summer.

   _____

   _____

(continued)

3. You can serve turkey for the holiday dinner. You can serve ham.

_____

_____

4. Naoto loves to celebrate New Year's Eve. He's too sick to go out this year.

_____

_____

5. Poinsettias are popular plants at Christmas. They bloom in the winter.

_____

_____

6. The Easter egg isn't in plain view. It isn't completely hidden.

_____

_____

7. Katia and her family celebrate Pushkin's birthday. He was a great Russian poet.

_____

_____

8. Peiya doesn't like fireworks. She watches them with her children.

_____

_____

9. Mexican children love skeleton candy. They look forward to Día de los Muertos.

_____

_____

Paragraph Format

When you write a paragraph in English, you must use correct paragraph format. Read the rules for paragraph format in the list below. Then, look at the diagram. Put the number of the appropriate rule in the square(s).

1. Put your name and the date in the upper righthand corner.
2. Center your title on the next line.
3. Indent the first sentence by using the tab key or by going in five spaces to the right.
4. Start each sentence with a capital letter.
5. End each sentence with a period, a question mark, or an exclamation point.
6. Begin each sentence where the previous sentence ends.
7. Write on every other line. This is called double-spacing.
8. Put margins of about one inch on each side of the paper.

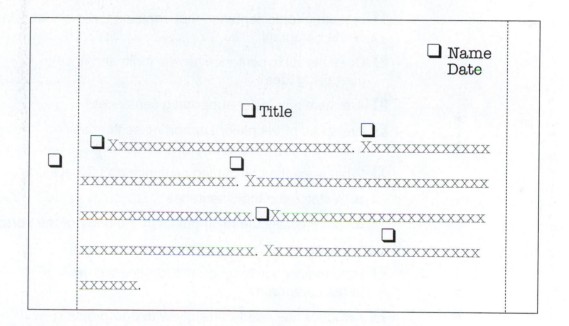

Some teachers accept handwritten papers, but many prefer that you do your work on a computer. There are additional considerations for writing on the computer, which you can find in Appendix 3 on page 178.

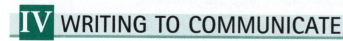

IV WRITING TO COMMUNICATE

Your Turn

You have learned a lot about paragraphs in this chapter. Now you are ready to write your own paragraph. Look back at Practice 3 on page 5. Choose one of the holidays for which you wrote a topic sentence, or choose another holiday that you know about. Write a topic sentence, the supporting sentences, and a concluding sentence. Be sure to use good paragraph format.

Paragraph Checklist

Use this paragraph checklist as a reminder of everything that you need to have in a paragraph. Check off (✔) the items that are true. If any of the items are *not* checked off and you need them, correct your paragraph and then complete the checklist.

CONTENT

What does the body of the paragraph consist of? (Check all that apply.)

   a. facts . . . . ❑

   b. examples . . . . ❑

   c. an illustration based on personal experience . . . . ❑

ORGANIZATION

1 Is there a topic sentence that contains the main idea
of the paragraph? . . . . ❑

2 Does the topic sentence have a topic and a
controlling idea? . . . . ❑

3 Are there any major supporting sentences? . . . . ❑

4 Are some of the major supporting sentences
explained by minor supporting sentences? . . . . ❑

5 What does the concluding sentence do? (Check one.)

   a. restates the topic sentence . . . . ❑

   b. summarizes the main points of the body of the paragraph . . . ❑

MECHANICS

1 How many coordinating conjunctions are used
in the paragraph? _____

2 Are commas used correctly with coordinating
conjunctions? . . . . ❑

Writing to Communicate . . . More

For more writing practice, choose one of these assignments.

1. Choose another holiday from your country and write about it.
2. Explain how your family celebrates a certain holiday.
3. Write about a holiday celebration that you remember.
4. Make up a new holiday and explain how to celebrate it.

CHAPTER 2

CHARACTERISTICS OF GOOD WRITING

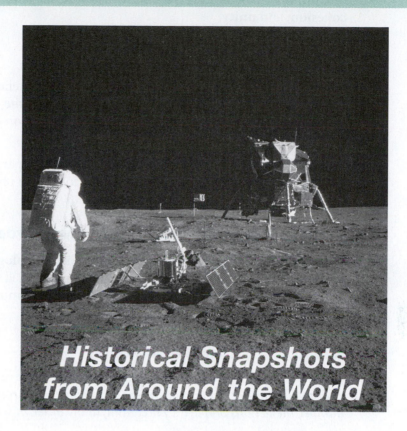

Historical Snapshots from Around the World

I VOCABULARY BUILDER

Below is a chart with verbs that you can use to talk about the history of a country. Work with a classmate to fill in the past tense form and the past participle form.

Verb	Past Form	Past Participle	Verb	Past Form	Past Participle
begin	*began*	*has begun*	lead		
bring			lose		
build			make		
buy			ride		
come			spread		
descend			say		
establish			take		
fall			think		
feel			wear		
grow			write		

In Chapter 1, you learned that a well-written paragraph has three separate parts: a topic sentence, supporting sentences, and a concluding sentence. In addition to organization, writing in English must also have the characteristics of **coherence**, **cohesion**, and **unity**.

Coherence

A paragraph has **coherence** when the supporting sentences are ordered according to a principle. The sentences are put in order so that the reader can understand your ideas easily. The principles for ordering depend on the type of paragraph you are writing.

There are three main types of paragraphs. **Narrative** paragraphs tell a story, **descriptive** paragraphs tell what something looks like physically, and **expository** paragraphs explain something.

Narrative Paragraphs and Chronological Ordering

For a narrative paragraph, you must use good **chronological ordering** of sentences. This means that the supporting sentences tell the events of a story in the order that they happened. In other words, the events must be ordered according to **time**. Another order might confuse the reader.

■ PRACTICE 1: Chronological Ordering

The following paragraph tells about an important event in the history of the world. It clearly tells the story of that one event as it happened through time. As you read, number the actions on page 19 according to the order in which Armstrong took them.

Model Paragraph 1

A Walk on the Moon

July 21, 1969, was an unforgettable day for all the citizens of planet Earth, particularly Neil Armstrong. After traveling for three days, the Apollo 11 spacecraft landed on the moon. Before Armstrong descended the ladder, he got dressed in his space suit. The entire world was watching when he opened the door of the Apollo 11 lunar module[1] and descended the ladder. He put his right foot on the moon's surface. Next he said the now-famous phrase, "One small step for a man, one giant leap for mankind." Then his fellow astronaut Buzz Aldrin joined him. Together, they performed scientific experiments and also had some fun entertaining the world with their lunar antics.[2] Since that day, several other people have walked on the moon, but none inspired a whole world in quite the same way.

[1]**module** *n.* a part of a spacecraft that can be separated from the main part and be used for a particular purpose

[2]**antics** *n.* behavior that seems strange, funny, silly, or annoying

____ descended the ladder	____ performed scientific experiments
____ got dressed in his space suit	____ prepared to take a step on the moon
____ had some fun entertaining the world	____ put his right foot on the moon's surface
____ opened the door of the *Apollo 11* lunar module	____ said the now-famous phrase, "One small step for a man, one giant leap for mankind."

Descriptive Paragraphs and Spatial Ordering

A descriptive paragraph paints a picture with words so that readers can picture in their minds the object or place you're describing. To make this easy for your readers, use **spatial ordering**. In other words, describe your object as it appears in **space**—when you are looking directly at it. Describe it from top to bottom, from left to right, from right to left, or from front to back.

■ PRACTICE 2: Spatial Ordering

In the model paragraph below, a flag is described from left to right and from top to bottom. Read the paragraph and then circle the picture of the flag on page 20 that is being described.

Model Paragraph 2

The Liberian Flag

The flag of Liberia, an African country established in 1842, is simple in its design. Overall, the flag is a rectangle approximately twice as wide as it is high. In the upper left-hand corner is a square of dark blue, which stands for Africa. The square is a little less than a sixth of the entire flag. On the square of blue, there is one star. This star has five points and symbolizes the fact that Liberia was the first independent republic in Africa. The rest of the flag has eleven stripes[1] of red and white. Each stripe represents one of the original signers of Liberia's constitution. On the right side of the blue square, there are five stripes. Under the blue square are six stripes. The top stripe of the flag is red, and the bottom one is, too. In short, this straightforward[2] design of the Liberian flag has not changed since 1847, when it was first flown for the new nation.

[1]**stripe** *n.* a long narrow line of color   [2]**straightforward** *n.* not complicated

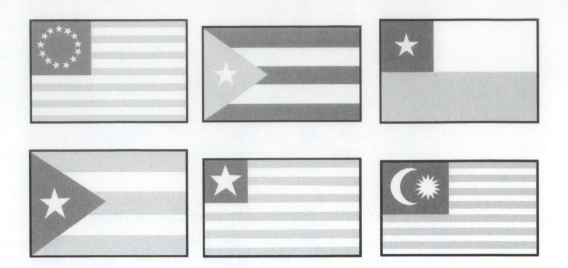

Expository Paragraphs and Logical Ordering

Expository paragraphs also require good coherence. The principle, however, is different. With expository paragraphs, coherence is based on **logic** or **reason**. This is called **logical ordering**. The ordering of the supporting sentences follows a logical pattern of major supporting sentences and minor supporting sentences.

Unlike time or space, logic depends on a person's view, so the ordering of supporting sentences is not as strict. You as the writer make decisions about what is a logical way of presenting your ideas.

Model Paragraph 3

Early Environmentalism[1]

The idea of environmentalism in the United States really started in the 1900s with two prominent[2] nature lovers. First, there was Henry David Thoreau. Thoreau lived for a short time in the woods by Walden Pond in Massachusetts. The book he wrote about his experience was published in 1854 and put forth the idea of natural living. The second person to bring attention to nature was John Muir. His travels and experiences in the western part of the United States, especially in California's Yosemite Valley, led him to form the country's first environmental organization. It was called the Sierra Club and is still very active today in preserving nature. In short, we can thank Henry David Thoreau and John Muir for starting the environmental movement[3] in the United States.

[1]**environmentalism** *n.* the idea of protecting the Earth

[2]**prominent** *adj.* important

[3]**movement** *n.* the work of a group of people trying to achieve a goal

> **What about you?**
>
> What environmental organizations are working in your country? Tell your classmates about them.

■ **PRACTICE 3: Diagramming a Paragraph**

Diagram Model Paragraph 3 above. Look at page 8 to review how to diagram a paragraph.

In your diagram, you should have identified two major supporting sentences: *First, there was Henry David Thoreau* and *The second person to bring attention to nature was John Muir.* The writer of this paragraph thought that it was logical to discuss Thoreau before discussing Muir. However, another writer might have decided to first talk about Muir and then Thoreau. Both orderings are possible because logic is not always the same to people.

■ PRACTICE 4: Working with Coherence

Identify each of these paragraphs as narrative (N), descriptive (D), or expository (E). Write the correct letter on the line after the number. Then circle the sentence that is out of order and draw an arrow to indicate where it should go.

1. ____

Native Wampanoag Clothes

The Wampanoag people, the native people who greeted the first settlers to North America in the 1600s, wore functional[1] clothing with few decorations. A Wampanoag man usually wore a feather in his long hair. On his feet, especially in the winter, he wore elk-skin moccasins.[2] His shirt was short-sleeved and made of deerskin. In cold weather, a robe of beaver fur covered his shoulders as well. Around his neck, he wore necklaces made from bones, shells, and claws.[3] His underwear was made from skunk fur, but his leggings[4] were made from deerskin. The ties that kept the leggings up were made from hemp grown in the area. All in all, the first sightings of the Wampanoag revealed a very practically dressed people.

[1]**functional** *adj.* designed to be useful rather than attractive
[2]**moccasin** *n.* a flat, comfortable shoe made of soft leather
[3]**claw** *n.* a sharp, curved nail on an animal
[4]**leggings** *n.* socks that cover your leg

elk   deer   beaver   skunk

2. _____

Brasília

Brasília, the capital of Brazil, is a good example of a planned city. First of all, the government of Brazil wanted to establish a capital city in the heart of the country and hired Lúcio Costa to design the city. The construction happened quickly because workers came from every part of Brazil to build the city. Costa envisioned[1] the city in the shape of a cross, with wide avenues dividing parts of the city. Indeed, from the sky looking down, Brasília actually looks like an airplane or a bird with opened wings. Moreover, Brasília was intended as a place where the different peoples and cultures of Brazil could come together. It was built in less than four years, and it was officially inaugurated[2] on April 21, 1960. Today, Brasília is a thriving city, where people from around the country have come to establish their own culture. In short, Brazilians are understandably proud of their capital city, Brasília.

[1]**envision** v. to imagine something as a future possibility

[2]**inaugurate** v. to open a new building or start a new service with a ceremony

3. _____

The Accidental Discovery

Louis Pasteur, the famous French scientist, unintentionally[1] discovered the principles of vaccination[2] against diseases. In 1879, while he was studying the disease of cholera,[3] he injected[4] some chickens with samples of the disease. He thought that he was using a recent sample of cholera, but it was an old sample. The chickens got sick, but then they recovered. Later, he injected them again with a sample that he knew was recent. The chickens were supposed to die, but they didn't. Pasteur was surprised when none of the chickens even got sick. In conclusion, Louis Pasteur, without knowing it, discovered that an old sample of a disease, used as a vaccination, can prevent the disease.

[1]**unintentionally** adv. not done deliberately; done by accident

[2]**vaccination**, n. a protection from a disease

[3]**cholera** n. a serious infectious disease that attacks the stomach and bowels

[4]**inject** v. to put a liquid, especially a drug, into your body by using a special needle

Cohesion

Another characteristic of a good paragraph is **cohesion**. When a paragraph has cohesion, all the supporting sentences connect to each other in their support of the topic sentence. The methods of connecting sentences to each other are called **cohesive devices**. Four important cohesive devices are **connectors**, **definite articles**, **personal pronouns**, and **demonstrative pronouns**.

Connectors

There are many kinds of connectors that provide cohesion. In other chapters, you will learn more about these connectors, such as **coordinating conjunctions** (discussed in Chapter 1), **subordinating conjunctions** (discussed in Chapter 3), **transitions** (discussed in Chapter 4), and **prepositions** (discussed in Chapter 5).

The Definite Article

A second way to connect sentences is to use the definite article *the*. A noun with a definite article often relates to a previously mentioned noun. For example:

➤ I bought a history book yesterday.

➤ I needed *the* history book for my classes.

It's obvious that these two sentences are talking about the same history book because of the definite article in the second sentence. In fact, if the definite article were not used, these two sentences would not be related. Look at these two sentences:

➤ I bought a history book yesterday.

➤ I needed *a* history book for my classes.

■ PRACTICE 5: Finding the Definite Article

Look back at the paragraph "The Liberian Flag" on page 19. Circle all of the definite articles.

Personal Pronouns

Another way to help a paragraph have good cohesion is by using personal pronouns. A pronoun usually refers back to a previous noun—its **antecedent**. For example:

➤ John is a history teacher.

➤ *He* just got a job at the local high school.

Using the personal pronoun *he* in the second sentence connects these two sentences. In fact, if you didn't use pronouns, you would have a second sentence that might not seem related to the first one. For example:

➤ John is a history teacher.

➤ *John* just got a job at the local high school.

■ **PRACTICE 6:** Finding Personal Pronouns

Look back at the paragraph "A Walk on the Moon" on page 18. Circle each of the personal pronouns. Then draw an arrow back to its antecedent.

Demonstrative Adjectives and Pronouns

Another way to provide cohesion is to use the demonstrative adjectives and pronouns *this, that, these,* and *those.* Like previous cohesive devices, they require antecedents in order to help connect sentences to those that came before. For example:

➤ The history of the Wampanoag people is typical.

➤ **These** people lost land and their way of life.
demonstrative adjective

➤ The Wampanoag people lost their way of life.

➤ **This** was tragic.
demonstrative pronoun

You could also use the definite article instead of the demonstrative pronoun to indicate that the two sentences go together. However, you must use one or the other. If you don't, then these two sentences aren't connected. For example:

➤ The history of the Wampanoag people is typical.

➤ People lost land and their way of life.

■ **PRACTICE 7:** Working with Cohesive Devices

The paragraph below lacks cohesion because it doesn't have connectors, definite articles, personal pronouns, or demonstrative pronouns. Rewrite the paragraph on a separate piece of paper. Make the cohesion better by:

● adding this transition: *in short*

● using a pronoun for the underlined parts

● using the definite article or a demonstrative pronoun for the double underlined parts

The Pony Express

In 1860, Pony Express riders were loved because <u>Pony Express riders</u> delivered mail in the United States relatively quickly, but <u>Pony Express riders'</u> job was very difficult. A typical day for a Pony Express rider began before sunrise. <u>A</u> Pony Express rider took a mail bag and rode at a horse's full speed for twenty-five miles to a station. Then, <u>Pony Express rider</u> jumped off <u>a</u> horse and jumped on another horse, still carrying <u>a</u> mail bag. There was no time for <u>a</u> <u>Pony Express rider</u> to stop and talk or even eat. Next, <u>Pony Express</u> rider had to ride another twenty-five miles to <u>a</u> next station. At <u>a</u> point, <u>a Pony Express</u> rider was only two-thirds finished with <u>a</u> trip. By the end of the day, <u>a Pony Express rider</u> had to cover seventy-five miles. Only then could <u>a Pony Express rider</u> rest and eat and get ready for <u>a</u> next day. A Pony Express rider's job was exhausting.

Unity

The final characteristic of a well-written paragraph is **unity**. All the supporting sentences should relate to the topic sentence. The following paragraph is a description of Pha That Luang, a Laotian monument. All the supporting sentences should be part of the description, but one sentence is not. A sentence that does not belong in a paragraph is called an **irrelevant sentence**.

Find the irrelevant sentence in this paragraph and cross it out.

A National Treasure

Pha That Luang is a beautiful monument to the independence of the Laotian people. On top of a hill in the capital city, Pha That Luang can be seen for miles. In fact, when I first saw it, I was at least 10 miles away. Its base is a square with four walls that look like large lotus[1] petals. At each corner is a stupa,[2] and there is one gate on each of the four sides. The gates open onto stairs that take you to the second level. The second level is another smaller square with 30 stupas surrounding it. The third level has the grandest stupa in the middle. It reaches 45 meters from the base of the monument to its top. It is shaped like a long lotus bud, and on top of it is a decoration that looks like a banana flower with an umbrella on its top. The whole monument is covered in shining gold leaf.[3] Indeed, Pha That Luang truly is a treasure for the Laotian people.

---

[1]**lotus** *n.* a type of flower

[2]**stupa** *n.* a type of Buddhist structure with a long upright spire

[3]**gold leaf** *n.* gold that has been beaten into extremely thin sheets and is used to cover things

Find the irrelevant sentences and cross them out so that the paragraph will be unified. Note that there may be more than one in each paragraph. Discuss with a classmate why the sentences are irrelevant.

1.

Two Similar Canals

The Suez Canal and the Panama Canal have similar histories. Today, many tourists visit both canals. The same Frenchman, Ferdinand de Lesseps, controlled the initial building of both canals. The Suez Canal was begun in 1859 by the Suez Canal Company. This company, which completed the project in 1869, was controlled by the French. Likewise, the French bought a Colombian canal-building company in 1881 in order to build the Panama Canal. Although the French started the canal, the United States finally finished that canal in 1914. Before this, Panama gained its independence from Colombia. In the end, however, both canals finally came under control of the countries in which they are located. Egypt gained control of the Suez Canal in 1957 by fighting France and Britain. Panama gained control over its canal peaceably in 1977. These similar events took place about twenty years apart and provided the world with two important waterways.

2.

A Woman of Strength

The strength of character that Eleanor Roosevelt possessed was obvious in her face. On her head, which was always held high, her light hair was styled in a no-nonsense way and did not cover her forehead or eyes. Her eyebrows were thick, natural, and expressive. Under these were her intense eyes, which revealed her intelligent mind. Her nose was straight, and, as she aged, her cheeks sagged a bit and formed the common wrinkles that make a triangle out of the nose and edges of the mouth. She was a serious woman, but, when she smiled, her smile showed sincerity and genuine pleasure. She was a great asset to her husband, Franklin, who was president of the United States from 1932 to 1945. In short, it was clear from the first impression that Eleanor Roosevelt was a strong woman.

What about you?

Who are some famous women in your country's history? Why are they famous? What do they look like? Share your answers with a classmate.

3.

Learning from Mummies[1]

Mummies have provided archeologists with important information about past civilizations. For example, Tollund Man is a mummy that was found by farmers in Denmark in 1950. The mummy was so well preserved[2] that the farmers thought that they had uncovered a recent murder. In fact, Tollund Man lived over 2,000 years ago. His stomach contained the ingredients for a vegetable soup. Momia Juanita, found in Peru, is another mummy that was so well preserved that her internal organs[3] could be analyzed. Because of this, archeologists learned more about the health and nutrition of the Inca people 500 years ago. Another example is the Iceman, which was found in the Alps in 1991. This mummified man answered hundreds of questions about life in the region over 5,000 years ago. One of the most significant mummy discoveries was the Tarim mummies, which were found in central China. These mummies were of European, not Asian, descent.[4] This discovery suggested that there were trade routes between Asia and Europe thousands of years ago. Even today, there are communities, such as Summum, that practice mummification. Therefore, archeologists in the future will also have mummies to learn from. In short, archeologists love to find mummies and learn something new about the past.

[1]**mummy** *n.* a dead body that has been preserved and often wrapped in cloth

[2]**preserve** *v.* to keep something or someone from being harmed or destroyed

[3]**internal organ** *n.* a part of the inside of your body

[4]**descent** *n.* your family origins; the country your family came from

III STRUCTURE AND MECHANICS

Using Commas in Lists

In English writing, commas are usually used between all words or phrases in a list of more than two items. The items can be of any grammatical structure. The comma before the coordinating conjunction is considered optional in some lists of one-word items. For example:

➤ The Wampanoag man wore a necklace made from bones, shells and claws. *(nouns; no comma before the coordinating conjunction)*

➤ Eleanor Roosevelt's eyebrows were thick, natural, and expressive. *(adjectives; comma before the coordinating conjunction)*

➤ Neil Armstrong put his space suit on, descended the stairs, and stepped on the moon. *(verb phrases; comma before the coordinating conjunction)*

➤ On top of a hill, under a bright sun, in front of me stood Pha That Luang. *(prepositional phrases)*

Add commas to these sentences. Then identify the grammatical structure in each list.

1. Through the rain across the desert and over the mountains the Pony Express riders rode. _____

2. Abraham Lincoln grew up in Kentucky served as a congressman from Illinois and died as president in Washington, D.C. _____

3. Jill Rosa Louis Dana and I studied for the history exam last night. _____

4. Some of the most famous museums in Washington, D.C., are the National Air and Space Museum the National Gallery of Art and the National Museum of Natural History. _____

5. Like many scientists, Louis Pasteur was brilliant methodical and curious. _____

6. To unearth a mummy, an archeologist uses a small brush dusts away the dirt and uncovers the mummy one small part at a time. _____

7. A history class can be exciting fascinating and thought-provoking, or it can be boring dull and deadly, depending on the professor. _____

8. To find the museum, you need to go over the bridge across the park and through the rose garden. _____

IV WRITING TO COMMUNICATE

Your Turn

Imagine that you are in a world history class and that your professor wants you to write about an aspect of your country's history. Choose one of these assignments.

- Write about the life of an important person or inventor in your country's history.

- Describe an important building or monument in your country.

- Explain an important day, year, or decade in your country's history.

Paragraph Checklist

Use the following paragraph checklist as a reminder of everything that you need to have in a paragraph. Check off (✔) the items that are true. If any of the items are *not* checked off and you need them, correct your paragraph and then complete the checklist.

CONTENT

1 What kind of paragraph is it? (Check one.)

   a. narrative . . . . ❏

   b. descriptive . . . . ❏

   c. expository . . . . ❏

2 Does the paragraph have unity, with no irrelevant sentences? . . ❏

ORGANIZATION

1 Is there a topic sentence at the beginning of the paragraph? . . . ❏

2 What kind of ordering does the paragraph use? (Check one.)

   a. chronological ordering. . . . . ❏

   b. spatial ordering . . . . ❏

   c. logical ordering . . . . ❏

3 What kinds of cohesive devices are used? (Check all that apply.)

   a. connectors. . . . . ❏

   b. the definite article . . . . ❏

   c. personal pronouns. . . . . ❏

   d. demonstrative pronouns. . . . . ❏

MECHANICS

1 Is the paragraph formatted correctly, including
indentation and margins?. . . . . ❏

2 Are commas used correctly?

   a. with coordinating conjunctions. . . . . ❏

   b. in lists . . . . ❏

Writing to Communicate . . . More

For more writing practice, choose one of these assignments.

1. Describe a famous statue in your country.
2. Write about a trip that you took to learn about the history of your country.
3. Do you think that knowing about history is important? Why or why not?

THE WRITING PROCESS

School Days

I | VOCABULARY BUILDER

Below are ten subjects you may have studied in high school and ten typical activities in a classroom. Choose one word from the first column (for example, biology) and one phrase from the second column (for example, conduct an experiment) to create a sentence. Change the verb forms if necessary.

School Subject	Activities
biology	conduct an experiment
chemistry	copy notes
computer science	do an assignment
foreign languages	do homework
geography	give a presentation
history	give a recital
mathematics	play a sport
music	take a test
physical education	take an exam
physics	work with a group

1. _I enjoyed conducting experiments in my biology class._
2. _____
3. _____
4. _____

II WRITING FOCUS

The Writing Process

In the first two chapters, you studied the organization of the basic building block of English academic writing: the paragraph. You also learned about the essential characteristics of a good paragraph. In this chapter, you will focus on the **process of writing**. You will continue to work on writing a stand-alone paragraph, but the process you will practice in this chapter is exactly the same for writing of any length.

There are six steps in the writing process:

1. analyzing the assignment
2. brainstorming
3. organizing your ideas
4. writing the first draft
5. rewriting the first draft
6. writing the next (or final) draft

These steps follow each other in order, but it is also very common to repeat some of the stages multiple times. This is particularly true with writing the first draft and writing the next draft. Below is a diagram showing the writing process.

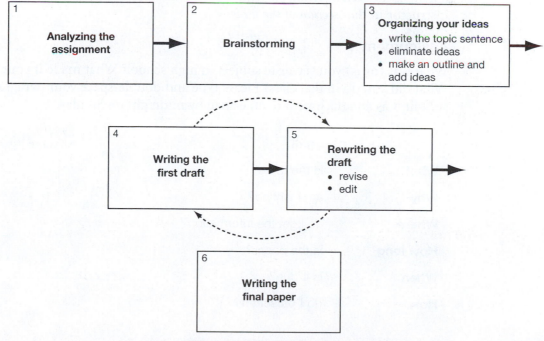

Diagram 1: The Writing Process

Step 1: Analyzing the Assignment

The first step is to be sure that you understand the assignment. You want to give your instructor what is asked for. For example, your instructor gives you this assignment:

Write a well-organized paragraph giving advice to a person who wants to learn a foreign language. Use your own knowledge. Please submit your paragraph by noon on Monday. I will only accept typed papers.

You should ask yourself the following questions: **what**, **why**, **where**, **how long**, **when**, and **how**.

Question		Answer (for this assignment)
What	is the topic?	Advice for learning a foreign language
Why	am I writing?	To show my ability to organize a concept
Where	do I get the information?	From what I already know
How long	is the paper?	One paragraph
When	is it due?	Monday at noon
How	do I present it?	Typed

Diagram 2: Analyzing the Assignment

■ PRACTICE 1: Analyzing Assignments

Below are three assignments that an instructor might give you. Read them and complete the chart below each assignment. You may not be able to answer all six questions for each assignment. When you cannot answer a question, write Ask the instructor *in that section of the table.*

Assignment 1

What was (or is) your favorite subject in high school? What made it your favorite? What did you do in that class? Please type and double-space your paragraph and submit it as an attachment to an e-mail by midnight on Sunday.

Question		Answer
What	is the topic?	
Why	am I writing?	
Where	do I get the information?	
How long	is the paper?	
When	is it due?	
How	do I present it?	

Assignment 2

Are you for or against school uniforms? Write a single paragraph giving at least three examples that support your opinion.

	Question	Answer
What	is the topic?	
Why	am I writing?	
Where	do I get the information?	
How long	is the paper?	
When	is it due?	
How	do I present it?	

Assignment 3

The school newspaper is collecting students' opinions on methods of studying for an exam. Write a paragraph describing the best ways to study for a big test, supporting your opinion with examples from your own experience. Please e-mail your paragraph to the newspaper editor at editor@schoolpaper.edu by next Monday at noon.

	Question	Answer
What	is the topic?	
Why	am I writing?	
Where	do I get the information?	
How long	is the paper?	
When	is it due?	
How	do I present it?	

Step 2: Brainstorming

To "brainstorm" means to write down ideas of all kinds—good or bad—on a piece of paper. Don't evaluate the ideas at this stage because in brainstorming all ideas are equal. You will evaluate at the next stage.

It is very helpful to work with a group of classmates when you are searching for ideas for a writing assignment, but, of course, you don't always have a group available. The next activities can be done both in groups and alone.

Using a Mind Map

Start with a circle in the middle of a piece of paper. Write the topic of the assignment inside the circle. Then start adding ideas you associate with this topic around the circle. You can use lines to point to the various ideas, you can use arrows to show that ideas are related, or you can put related ideas in smaller circles. In other words, there is no right or wrong way.

For example, the topic from Assignment 1 on page 32 is about a student's favorite class. This diagram is an example of this technique.

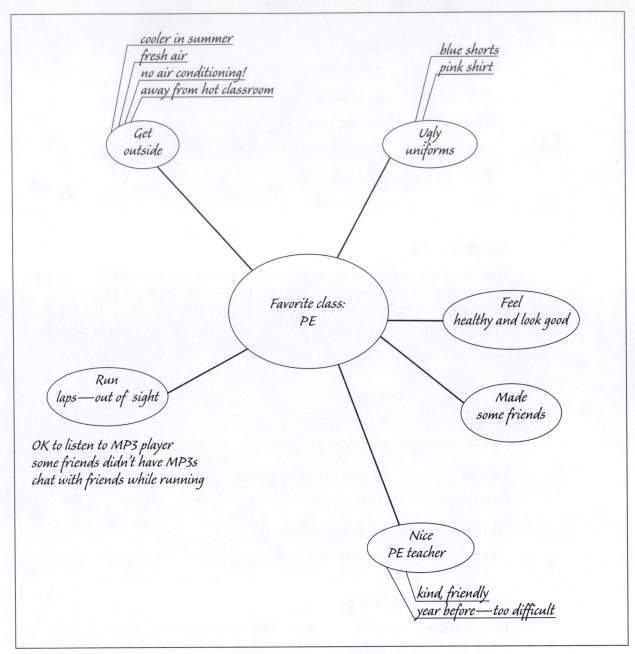

cooler in summer
fresh air
no air conditioning!
away from hot classroom

Get
outside

blue shorts
pink shirt

Ugly
uniforms

Favorite class:
PE

Feel
healthy and look good

Run
laps—out of sight

Made
some friends

OK to listen to MP3 player
some friends didn't have MP3s
chat with friends while running

Nice
PE teacher

kind, friendly
year before—too difficult

Diagram 3: Using a Mind Map

Using Columns

To use this technique, fold a piece of paper lengthwise in two, three, or four to create two, three, or four columns. Write the general topic, *favorite class* at the top of the paper. Then, write a key word—of any kind—at the top of each column. Now start writing down all kinds of words that come to mind under the heading in each column.

Here is a sample of this technique:

Favorite class—physical education		
Reason	*Example*	*Details*
get out of classroom	always hot in classroom!	no AC!
could choose to run laps	chance to chat with friends	met some friends
PE teacher	kind	nicer than history
	friendly	teacher
		lets us use MP3
PE uniforms ugly	blue shorts, pink shirt	nobody looked good
		in them
Need exercise!!!!!!	feel good	strong muscles
	look good	can do more things
		learned more sports

Diagram 4: Using Columns

Freewriting

Start with a word or a phrase and write down anything you can think of that is related to the topic. Instead of listing a lot of points, try to write complete sentences. When you get stuck, just start writing more about one of the previous words and continue writing about that. Don't worry about grammar, punctuation, or spelling because no one else will see your freewriting. The most important aspect of freewriting is *to not allow yourself to stop*. Just let your ideas and imagination flow. Here is an example of a freewriting exercise about the topic *Favorite high school subject*.

Don't worry about spelling, grammar, or punctuation. It's all right to make mistakes at this point. The purpose of freewriting is to get as many ideas as you can down on paper.

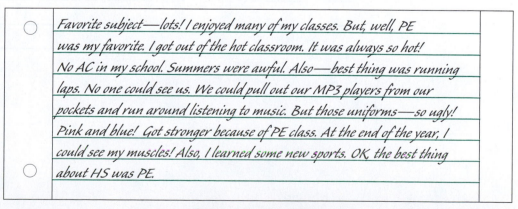

Favorite subject—lots! I enjoyed many of my classes. But, well, PE was my favorite. I got out of the hot classroom. It was always so hot! No AC in my school. Summers were awful. Also—best thing was running laps. No one could see us. We could pull out our MP3 players from our pockets and run around listening to music. But those uniforms—so ugly! Pink and blue! Got stronger because of PE class. At the end of the year, I could see my muscles! Also, I learned some new sports. OK, the best thing about HS was PE.

Diagram 5: Freewriting

Below are two of the assignments from Practice 1 on pages 32–33. With a classmate, choose one of these topics to practice brainstorming. While discussing the topic, one student should take notes using a mind map diagram, and the other student should take notes using a column diagram. Next, by yourself, for more practice with brainstorming, do a five-minute freewriting exercise by yourself on the other topic.

Assignment 2

Are you for or against school uniforms? Write a single paragraph giving at least three examples that support your opinion.

Assignment 3

The school newspaper is collecting students' opinions on methods of studying for an exam. Write a paragraph describing the best ways to study for a big test, supporting your opinion with examples from your own experience. Please e-mail your paragraph to the newspaper editor at editor@schoolpaper.edu by next Monday at noon.

Step 3: Organizing Your Ideas

You will probably find that you can write many different paragraphs from the ideas in your brainstorming. Now you need to organize your ideas. Step 3 has three stages:

● write your topic sentence

● eliminate irrelevant ideas

● make an outline and add relevant ideas

Writing Your Topic Sentence

You already have the topic, but you need to consider what your opinion about the topic is. In other words, choose your controlling idea. This may involve narrowing down the topic.

■ **PRACTICE 3: Choosing Controlling Ideas**

Refer to the mind map diagram on page 34. In pairs or small groups, write topic sentences with different controlling ideas. Notice that for each controlling idea you choose, you will only need <u>some</u> of the words. The first one is done for you.

1. *Physical education is great because you need exercise.* _____

2. _____

3. _____

Eliminating Irrelevant Ideas

You probably cannot use all the ideas that you have generated from your brainstorming in your paragraph. As you know, a paragraph has to have unity. Therefore, after you have written your topic sentence, eliminate the ideas you don't need.

■ PRACTICE 4: Eliminating Irrelevant Ideas

Look again at the mind map on page 34. Here is a topic sentence for this topic:

➤ PE was my favorite class in high school for a lot of reasons.

Some of the ideas in the diagram are irrelevant to the controlling idea of this topic sentence. For example, "ugly uniforms" is not relevant to the topic sentence. Cross out other irrelevant ideas in the mind map. Then compare your decisions with a classmate. Did you cross out the same ideas? If not, discuss why you made different decisions.

Making an Outline and Adding Relevant Ideas

You might need to add more ideas to the ones you have selected. These additional ideas may become another major supporting sentence or a minor supporting sentence to a major supporting sentence you already have.

A good way to add relevant ideas is to make an outline. You don't have to use complete sentences. All you need are a few words to help you remember what you are going to write. Like brainstorming, an outline is just for you, so you don't need to worry about grammar.

Here is a sample of a conventional outline. Label the items in this outline as **TS** (topic sentence), **SS** (major supporting sentence), **ss** (minor supporting sentence), or **CS** (concluding sentence).

○	PE was my favorite class in high school for a lot of reasons.
	I. Reason—classroom was stuffy and hot
	A. Awful in summer—no AC
	B. fresh air outside
	II. Reason—running is great
	A. No one could see us
○	B. Play music
	C. Chat with friends
	III. Reason—feel healthier
	A. stronger
	B. sleep better (new idea)
	IV. Reason—PE teacher nice
	A. encouraging (new idea)
	B. kind, friendly
○	My PE class was a wonderful part of high school.

Diagram 6: Topic Outline

In Practice 2 on page 36, you brainstormed ideas for two assignments. Choose one of those assignments and write an outline. Go through all the parts of this procedure:

- write a topic sentence
- eliminate irrelevant ideas
- make an outline
- add relevant ideas

Step 4: Writing the First Draft

Now you are ready to turn the ideas in your outline into complete sentences and write the sentences in good paragraph format. This draft of your paragraph is just for you, so again, don't worry too much about grammar or punctuation. Here is the first draft of the paragraph about the student's favorite class.

My favorite high school class was phys ed for a lot of reasons. My school was in the city and it was always hot in the summer. We never had air conditioning. Secondly, we were allowed to run laps instead of other things. So we ran around where no one could see us. And the PE teacher was so nice! Encouraging, too. We played our MP3s and chatted while we were running. It was great. Next I felt healthier and stronger—even slept better! My PE class was a wonderful part of high school.

Diagram 7: First Draft

Step 5: Rewriting the First Draft

The next step is to rewrite your paragraph. Rewriting consists of two parts: **revising** and **editing**.

Revising

When you revise a paragraph, you check the organization of your paragraph and look at your ideas. Ask yourself questions like these:

- Does the paragraph have unity?
- Are there enough minor supporting ideas for the major supporting sentences?
- Do the supporting sentences have good coherence?
- Is there good cohesion?

Editing

When you edit a paragraph, look at the grammar, spelling, word forms, and punctuation. Since many of your editing mistakes may be eliminated when you revise your paragraph, you should always edit your writing *after* you revise it.

Look again at the first draft of the paragraph. Note the points for revision and editing that the writer has made. Can you think of any others?

Need title

physical education

My favorite high school class was phys ed for a

lot of reasons. ⌃ My school was in the city and it was
add transition   *not clear*
always hot in the summer. We never had air   *reason*

conditioning. Secondly, we were allowed to run laps
                                        Therefore,
instead of other things. ~~So~~ ⌃ we ran around where no
                        Add other reasons?
one could see us. ⌃ And the PE teacher was so nice!
Not complete sentence
Encouraging, too. We played our MP3s and chatted

while we were running. It was great. Next I felt ⟵ *move to*
                                                                                       second point
                                              In short,
healthier and stronger—even slept better! ⌃ My PE

class was a wonderful part of high school.

Diagram 8: First Draft Notes for Rewriting

Step 6: Writing the Final Paper (or Next Draft)

The last step in the writing process is to write a clean version of the paragraph with all the revisions and editing carried out. This draft is the one that you will turn in, so be sure that you use good paragraph format. Here is the final draft of the paragraph.

Chris Young
December 5, 2007

Physical Education

My favorite high school class was physical education for a lot of reasons. First of all, my school was in the city, and it was always too hot in the classroom. Going outside to the fresh air was such a relief. Secondly, in physical education, we were allowed to run laps instead of lifting weights or playing basketball. Therefore, we ran around where no one could see us. We could listen to our MP3 players and chat with friends as long as we were running. Moreover, the PE teacher was great. He was so kind and encouraging. I needed that. Finally, I felt so much healthier, and I even started sleeping better. In short, my PE class was a wonderful part of high school for me.

Diagram 9: Final Draft

Adverbial Clauses

Using Adverbial Clauses

An adverbial clause is a type of dependent clause. Using an adverbial clause makes your writing more sophisticated. To make an adverbial clause from an independent clause, use a **subordinating conjunction**.

Example 1

➤ Joe has always loved to read. He studied literature in college.

To show that one sentence is the cause of the other one, you can use the subordinator **because** or **since**.

➤ **Because** Joe has always loved to read, he studied literature in college.

➤ **Since** Joe has always loved to read, he studied literature in college.

Example 2

➤ Joe liked playing sports. Joe wasn't very good at it.

To show surprise that Joe isn't good at sports, you can use **even though** or **although**.

➤ **Even though** Joe liked playing sports, he wasn't very good at it.

➤ **Although** Joe liked playing sports, he wasn't very good at it.

As with transitions, there are many subordinators. Here are some of the most common ones.

Chronology	Causation	Unexpected Result	Difference	Condition
after	because	although	whereas	if
as	since	even though	while	
before				
until				
when				
while				

Comma Use with Adverbial Clauses

As shown in the examples above, when a sentence begins with an adverbial clause, there must be a comma between this clause and the independent clause. However, with most subordinators, when the adverbial clause comes after the independent clause, do not use a comma.

➤ Joe studied literature in college **because** he has always loved to read.

➤ Joe studied literature in college **since** he has always loved to read.

There is one exception to this rule. When an adverbial clause beginning with the subordinators *while* or *whereas* comes after an independent clause, you still use a comma.

➤ Joe is tall, **while** his brother is short.

➤ Joe is tall, **whereas** his brother is short.

Using Pronouns with Adverbial Clauses

In general, you use the full noun in whichever clause comes first and a pronoun in the second clause.

➤ **Mary** loves **her old school** even though **her** neighbors want to tear **it** down.

➤ Although **Mary's neighbors** attended **the old school**, **they** want to tear **it** down.

■ PRACTICE 6: Combining Clauses

Combine the pairs of sentences by making one an adverbial clause. Vary the position of the adverbial clause and use a comma when necessary. Remember to use a pronoun in the second part of the sentence if necessary.

1. Alex owns five bicycles. Alex bought another last week.

   _____

2. Teachers forbid students to use cell phones in class. Some students still use them.

   _____

3. Oscar thinks that chemistry class is great. Ruth thinks that it's awful.

   _____

4. Tanya didn't study for the history test. Tanya failed it.

   _____

5. The teacher is sick (maybe). We won't have the test.

   _____

6. The old school building is dangerous. The old building needs to be torn down.

   _____

7. Patricia woke up late. Patricia didn't miss her first class.

   _____

8. The school soccer team lost the match. No one at school was happy.

   _____

Your Turn

Below are three assignments on the topic of high school experiences. Choose the assignment that interests you the most. Form a group with other students in your class who chose the same topic. Go through Step 1 (Analyzing the Assignment) and Step 2 (Brainstorming) of the writing process with your group. Then complete Steps 3 through 6 on your own.

1. Write a paragraph about your favorite high school teacher. What made this person special? Make sure to use good paragraph format. Submit the assignment typed and double-spaced. You may type your assignment or write it by hand.

2. In most high schools the students form groups based on similar interests. What groups were there in your high school? Were there any problems because of the groups? Which group did you belong to and why? Write a well-organized paragraph describing the groups. Make sure to give plenty of examples. You may type your assignment or write it by hand.

3. What was the subject you liked least in high school? Why didn't you like it? Has that experience changed your life in any way? Write a paragraph describing the subject, the reasons for disliking it, and how it has influenced your life. Make sure to write clear topic and concluding sentences for your paragraph. You may type your assignment or write it by hand.

Peer Help Worksheet

You can use the peer help worksheet on page 44 as another way to revise and edit your paragraph. Trade paragraphs and textbooks with a classmate. Read your classmate's paragraph while your classmate reads yours. Check off (✔) the items in your partner's book as you evaluate them. Then return the paragraphs and books. If any of the items in your book are not checked off, and you agree with your partner, correct your paragraph before turning it in. Use a pencil if you write on your classmate's essay or book.

CONTENT

1 Is the writer's opinion in the topic sentence? . . . . ❑

2 Does the writer support his or her opinion? . . . . ❑

3 Does the paragraph have unity? . . . . ❑

If not, tell the writer about any sentences you think are irrelevant.

ORGANIZATION

1 Does the topic sentence have a clear topic and a clear
controlling idea? . . . . ❑

2 Do the supporting sentences have good coherence? . . . . ❑

3 What types of cohesive devices are used? (Check all that apply.)

   a. connectors . . . . ❑

   b. the definite article . . . . ❑

   c. pronouns . . . . ❑

   d. demonstrative pronouns . . . . ❑

4 What type of concluding sentence does this paragraph have?
(Check one.)

   a. summary . . . . ❑

   b. restatement of the topic sentence . . . . ❑

MECHANICS

Do you think sentences with adverb changes are punctuated
correctly? . . . . ❑

If not, discuss any possible mistakes with the writer.

Writing to Communicate . . . More

For more practice writing paragraphs, choose another one of these topics. Refer to
Appendix 1 on page 173 to review the writing process before you write.

1. The best way to study for a test
2. Your favorite after-school activity
3. Why learning a foreign language is useful

BRINGING IT ALL TOGETHER

I REVIEWING IDEAS

A. *Analyze the paragraph below by answering these questions.*

1. What is the topic sentence? Circle the topic and underline the controlling idea.

2. Does the paragraph have coherence? Put a circle around any sentence that is out of order, and draw an arrow to where it should be.

3. Does the paragraph have cohesion? Underline the cohesive devices (e.g., definite articles, pronouns).

4. Does the paragraph have unity? Cross out any irrelevant sentences.

5. What type of concluding sentence is in this paragraph? Check (✔) the answer.

 _____ a restatement   _____ a summary

Revolutions of the Sixties

The 1960s was a time of many social revolutions in the United States. First, there was the civil rights movement. This was started in the early sixties by the black people in the country, who were tired of being treated as second-class citizens. They demanded to be treated equally with the white majority. There are movies now about leaders such as Martin Luther King, Jr. and Malcolm X. Second, women learned from the civil rights movement and created a movement for themselves called women's liberation. Students began to question the policies of the United States and of the administration. They wanted to be paid the same salaries and have the same job opportunities as men, and they wanted to share the household tasks and the raising of children with the men in the their lives. Another social revolution in the sixties took place at colleges and universities. It was the time of the Vietnam War, and students on many campuses protested against the war by participating in marches and demonstrations. In conclusion, many social movements that affect U.S. society in important ways began in the 1960s.

B. Read the paragraph. Circle the correct connector in the parentheses below.

Celebrating the Fourth of July

A typical Fourth of July celebration in the United States can last all day long. In the morning, everyone goes downtown to see the parades. Children and politicians march down the street, (**so / and / but**) there are floats with the traditional red, white, and blue colors. (**While / Even though / After**) the parade is finished, the children look for their parents, (**for / nor / and**) the politicians give speeches. In the afternoon, family, friends, and neighbors come together to have a party. (**Since / If / Whereas**) July has very hot weather, the party is often near a pool, a lake, or the ocean. (**Because / Until / After**) it is dark, people enjoy colorful fireworks (**when / if / although**) the towns and cities all over the country put on their shows that light up the sky. In conclusion, Fourth of July days are long and fun-filled occasions to celebrate the country's independence.

II ERROR ANALYSIS

*Eight of the ten sentences below have comma mistakes in them. Write **C** (Correct) in the blank if the sentence has no mistakes. Write **I** (Incorrect) if the sentence has a mistake. Fix the incorrect sentences by adding or deleting commas, capital letters, and periods. Then compare your corrections with a classmate.*

_____ 1. Before you buy a big-screen television, you should do some research online.

_____ 2. The people of Chile celebrate Independence Day on September 18, and also remember the military takeover that took place on September 11, 1973.

_____ 3. Ellis Island in New York harbor has been used as an Army fort an Army storage area a first stop for immigrants to the United States and a museum.

_____ 4. Chinese New Year's parades are always fun to attend. If the weather is dry and it's not raining.

_____ 5. The first telephones were called "candlestick" telephones, for they had round heads, long candle-like stands, and circular bases.

_____ 6. My aunt collects cups saucers and spoons and she displays all of them in her breakfast room.

_____ 7. The old house on the beach had been empty for years. But, someone finally bought it last month.

_____ 8. Alex always invites his whole family for dinner on his birthday even though he'd really rather be alone.

_____ 9. Whereas the English arriving in North America in the 1600s believed in land ownership the native people did not think a person could own land.

_____ 10. Anna loves her new house, and never wants to move again.

THE ESSAY

CHAPTER 4

FROM PARAGRAPH TO ESSAY

Animals in Their Ecosystems

I VOCABULARY BUILDER

Habitats are defined as natural environments in which a plant or an animal lives. Habitats are located in ecosystems. Ecosystems are all the plants and animals in a particular area. In North America, there are five types of ecosystems: deserts, forests, grasslands, Arctic tundra, and wetlands.

A. *Look at the photos below. Match the animals on page 49 with their probable ecosystem by writing the appropriate habitat next to each animal photo.*

Habitats

wetlands

grasslands

Arctic tundra

desert

forest

Animals

polar bear _____

deer _____

buffalo _____

frog _____

rattlesnake _____

B. First, read this paragraph and pay attention to the bold words. Then, try to figure out what they mean.

Changing Habitats

At times, animals may find that their **ecosystem** can no longer support their **habitat**. It becomes no longer **sufficient** for their **survival** perhaps because there is not enough food or water or because it has become too dangerous. When this happens, individual animals must **seek** a new place to live. They may be able to **adapt** to other ecosystems if they can find a **suitable** habitat there. A deer, for example, which usually lives in forests, could live in grasslands if it learns to run fast enough to avoid its **predators**. Another example is the frog, which usually lives in wetlands. It may be able to adjust to living in a forest if it can find **shelter** and if the **climate** is damp enough. Changing habitats for these animals isn't easy, but it can be done.

What about you?

Which ecosystem would you prefer to visit? To live in? Explain your answers to a classmate.

C. Match each word to its definition by drawing a line from the word to its meaning.

adapt *v.*    all the animals and plants in a particular area

climate *n.*   to try to find something

ecosystem *n.*   enough

habitat *n.*   to change to fit a new situation

predator *n.*   a place where an animal can live safely

seek *v.*   right or acceptable for a certain situation

shelter *n.*   the typical weather conditions in an area

sufficient *adj.*   continuing to live or exist

suitable *adj.*   an animal that kills and eats other animals

survival *adj.*   a natural environment where an animal lives

II WRITING FOCUS

Expanding the Paragraph

As you have learned, a paragraph consists of three parts: a topic sentence, supporting sentences (the body), and a concluding sentence. Notice these three parts in Model Paragraph 1 below.

Model Paragraph 1

Man's Best Friend

There are three main relationships that people have with dogs. First, we have working dogs. These dogs, such as Siberian huskies and collies, serve people almost like employees. To a sheep farmer, for example, a good sheepdog is his most valuable partner. Other dogs are known primarily for their excellence in sports. The sleek[1] and extremely fast greyhound is used in dog races, and many hunting dogs, such as setters, retrievers, and pointers, often compete in hunting trials.[2] Third, many people enjoy dogs as companions. All kinds of dogs can be excellent companions, but a few breeds[3] are kept only for this purpose. Some examples are the toy dogs, such as Chihuahuas or Lhasa apsos. Because of the relationships they have with people, dogs are often called "man's best friend."

[1]**sleek** *adj.* smooth and healthy-looking

[2]**hunting trial** *n.* a competition where dogs get awards for excellent hunting behavior

[3]**breed** *n.* a type of animal

When you want to write about a topic in more detail, you can turn your paragraph into an **essay**. Similar to a paragraph, an essay is composed of three sections. These sections are the **introductory paragraph**; the **supporting paragraphs**, or the body; and the **concluding paragraph**. Paragraphs can be easily expanded to essay length. Here is Model Paragraph 1 expanded into an essay.

Model Essay 1

Man's Best Friend

The dog is generally considered the first domesticated[1] animal. It is believed that the direct ancestor[2] of the domestic dog is the wolf, originally found throughout Europe, Asia, and North America. Archeologists have found remains of dogs that are 10,000 years old. In these ancient societies, as well as in our modern one, there are three main relationships that people have with dogs.

First, there are working dogs. These dogs, such as Siberian huskies and collies, serve people almost like employees. The dogs help pull heavy loads, round up[3] cattle, and keep a sharp eye out for strangers. To a sheep farmer, for example, a good sheepdog is his most valuable partner. Sheepdogs, such as Border collies, standard collies, and Shetland sheepdogs, are very intelligent and can learn to respond to hand signals as well as spoken words. Sheepdogs in Scotland, for instance, move sheep along with just a glance from the farmer. As a result, working dogs know their worth to their master, and they are proud of it.

Other dogs are known primarily for their excellence in sports. For example, the sleek and extremely fast greyhound is used in dog races. These races take place on specially prepared tracks where the competitors[4] chase a mechanical rabbit. People gamble[5] on these athletes' performance. Next, special hunting dogs often compete in hunting trials. Bird dogs are a type of hunting dog. Setters and pointers, for example, recognize a bird's scent long before it makes a sound and show their owner where the bird is by standing very still. Retrievers, such as golden retrievers or Labrador retrievers, will throw themselves into an icy cold lake to pick up the bird their owner has shot. Clearly, sporting dogs are the athletes of the dog world.

(continued)

Third, many people enjoy dogs as companions. All kinds of dogs can be excellent friends. Both the working dogs and the hunting dogs have great patience and are very good with small children. Most of these dogs will allow children to climb all over them and are great baby-sitters because of their loyalty to their owner and their family. A few breeds are kept only for the purpose of being a companion. Some of these are the toy dogs, such as Chihuahuas or Lhasa apsos. Since these dogs are so tiny, they are great to have if you live in a small apartment. In short, all dogs, including the toy dogs, are wonderful companions.

In summary, although there are a great many breeds of dogs, they can be classified into these three main types by their relationships to their owners. Even if you have no interest in sports and no farm, you can have a great companion in a dog. Because of the relationships they have with people, dogs are often called "man's best friend."

What about you?

Are dogs popular in your country? Do you have a dog? Share your answers with a classmate.

[1]**domesticated** *adj.* referring to animals that live near people and are controlled by them

[2]**ancestor** *n.* a member of your family that lived in the past

[3]**round up** *v.* to find and gather together a group of people or things

[4]**competitor** *n.* someone or something trying to win

[5]**gamble** *v.* to risk money on the result of something like a dog race

Look at the diagram on page 53 to see how a paragraph is expanded into an essay.

- The topic sentence of the paragraph becomes the thesis statement of the essay, which comes at the end of the introductory paragraph.

- The supporting sentences of the original paragraph expand into three separate body paragraphs in the essay. In other words, each major supporting sentence and its minor supports in Model Paragraph 1 become one body paragraph in the corresponding essay.

- Finally, the concluding sentence is made into a concluding paragraph.

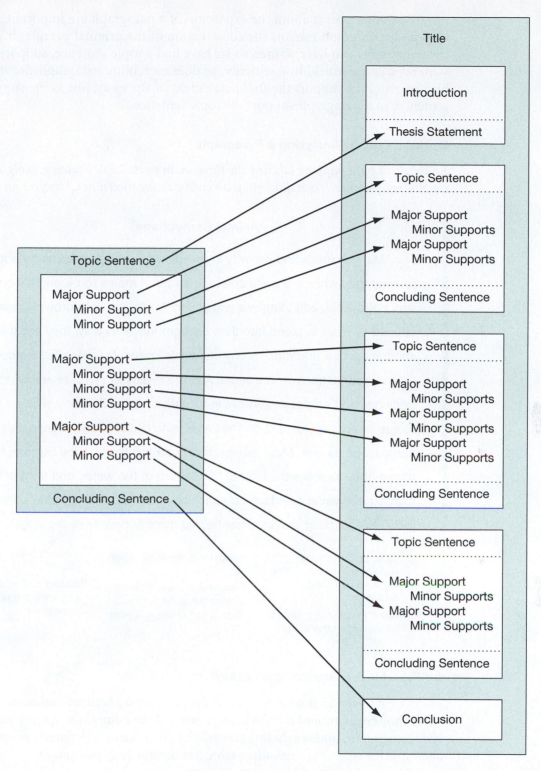

Diagram: Paragraph to Essay

Two other points about the expansion of a paragraph are important. First, each body paragraph mirrors the construction of the original paragraph. Just as the paragraphs you have written so far have had a topic sentence, supporting sentences, and a concluding sentence, so does each body paragraph. Second, the body paragraphs support the thesis statement of the essay, just as the supporting sentences in a paragraph support the topic sentence.

■ PRACTICE 1: Analyzing a Paragraph

Analyze this paragraph by labeling the three main parts: topic sentence, body, and concluding sentence. Then diagram it according to the model in Chapter 1 on page 8.

Animal Camouflage[1]

Many animals find security in blending in[2] with their environment. In birds, for example, while it is quite common for adult males to be brightly colored and very noticeable, adult females and young chicks are light brown or sand-colored in order to blend into their background. This way, they escape the sharp eyes of a predator.[3] Many mammals[4] have also adopted the colors of their surroundings over the years. A zebra is almost invisible among the branches and stripes of sunlight in its native Africa. Similarly, a lion is very hard to see when it is sleeping on the beige sand of the plains. Ocean dwellers[5] use camouflage as well. Most fish are darker on top than on the bottom; from above, they look like the land at the bottom of the water, and from below, they look like the water's surface. In conclusion, the safety that these animals' protective coloring provides has helped them survive over the ages.

[1]**camouflage** *n.* hiding something by making it look the same as the things around it

[2]**blend in** *v.* to mix in with, to be similar to other things

[3]**predator** *n.* a hunter, usually an animal

[4]**mammal** *n.* a warm-blooded animal that gives birth to live babies and drinks milk from its

mother's breast when it is young

[5]**dweller** *n.* a person or an animal that lives somewhere

■ PRACTICE 2: Analyzing an Essay

The essay on page 55 is an expansion of the paragraph about animal camouflage. First, draw boxes around the three components of the essay (introductory paragraph, body paragraphs, and concluding paragraph). Next, using a different-colored pen, underline the topic and concluding sentences in each body paragraph.

Animal Camouflage

Animals in the wild have many natural enemies. A small bird wants to avoid being seen by a hawk, a zebra doesn't want the lion to find him, and a flatfish would prefer that the shark swim quietly by. If an animal can't easily run away from its predator, how can it protect itself? One way that has evolved over time is protective coloring, or camouflage. Many animals find security in blending in with their environment.

In birds, for example, while adult males are brightly colored and very noticeable, adult females and young chicks are light brown or sand-colored in order to blend into their background and escape the sharp eyes of a predator. Consider the bright red cardinal, a very common bird in colder areas of North America. The male is bright and showy to attract a mate, but you hardly ever see the females. They are sandy brown, with touches of red on the wings, tail, and breast. The peacock is another bird where the male is bright and showy, while the female is easily overlooked because of her dull[1] coloring. The long tail feathers of the male are generally bright green and gold and have round markings of a rich color, known as peacock blue. The female, called a peahen, has short tail feathers and is much less colorful than the male. In short, adopting camouflage colors helps the female birds survive and raise another generation of birds.

Many mammals have also adopted the colors of their surroundings. A zebra is almost invisible[2] among the branches and stripes of sunlight in its native Africa because its black and white stripes mimic[3] the shadows among the trees and bushes. A lion is very hard to see when it is sleeping on the beige sand of the plains. The lioness, in particular, looks just like a part of the ground until she raises her head. The camouflage of the lioness makes her invisible to her prey,[4] so she can concentrate on hunting and feeding her young. All these mammals have, over many, many years, developed this protective coloring to assist them in the struggle to survive.

Ocean dwellers use camouflage as well. Most fish are darker on top than on the bottom; from above, they look like the land at the bottom of the water, and from below, they look like the water's surface. Many ocean fish have a horizontal[5] line along their body that separates the top from the bottom. An ocean mackerel, for example, is easily distinguished by this stripe. Some flatfish have taken this protection a step further; for example, a fish that lives on a sandy bottom has a light-brown upper side, while a flatfish that lives on a rocky bottom has an upper

(continued)

side that looks like pebbles. The result is, because they look just like their surroundings, these fish survive and avoid becoming someone else's lunch.

In summary, looking like their environment is helpful to these animals for the survival of the species.[6] The mother bird that is invisible among the brown leaves, the lion sleeping on the sandy plains, and the fish that hides among the pebbles will live to see another day. The safety these animals find in their protective coloring has helped them survive over the ages.

---

[1]**dull** *adj.* boring, unnoticeable, not bright or shiny

[2]**invisible** *adj.* not able to be seen

[3]**mimic** *v.* to copy the way someone or something is

[4]**prey** *n.* an animal that is hunted and eaten by another animal

[5]**horizontal** *adj.* flat, level, and straight; in the same direction as the horizon

[6]**species** *n.* a category of the classification of animals or plants

---

■ PRACTICE 3: Outlining an Essay

Here is part of an outline of the essay "Animal Camouflage." Complete the outline by writing in the key words from each paragraph of the essay.

I. Introductory paragraph

➤ *Thesis statement:* Many animals find security in blending in with their environment.

II. Body

A. Paragraph 1: Birds

➤ *Topic sentence:* In birds, for example, while adult males are brightly colored and very noticeable, adult females and young chicks are light brown or sand-colored in order to blend into their background and escape the sharp eyes of a predator.

Major support 1

➤ _____

Minor supports

➤ _____

➤ _____

Major support 2

➤ _____

Minor supports

➤ _____

➤ _____

➤ *Concluding sentence:* In short, adopting camouflage colors helps the female birds survive and raise another generation of birds.

B. Paragraph 2: Mammals

➤ *Topic sentence:* Many mammals have also adopted the colors of their surroundings.

  Major support 1

  ➤ _____

  Major support 2

  ➤ _____

  Major support 3

  ➤ _____

    Minor support

    ➤ _____

➤ *Concluding sentence:* All these mammals have, over many, many years, developed protective coloring to assist them in the struggle to survive.

C. Paragraph 3: Fish

➤ *Topic sentence:* Ocean dwellers use camouflage as well.

  Major support 1

  ➤ _____

    Minor supports

    ➤ _____

    ➤ _____

  Major support 3

  ➤ _____

➤ *Concluding sentence:* The result is, because they look just like their surroundings, these fish survive and avoid becoming someone else's lunch.

III. Concluding paragraph

➤ In summary, looking like their environment is helpful to these animals for the survival of the species. The mother bird that is invisible among the brown leaves, the lion sleeping on the sandy plains, and the fish that hides among the pebbles will live to see another day. The safety these animals find in their protective coloring has helped them survive over the ages.

III STRUCTURE AND MECHANICS

Using Transitions

Transitions are connectors that you use to make two sentences into one. There are many transition words and phrases in English. Here are some of the most common ones and their meanings. A more complete list is provided in Appendix 4 on pages 180–181.

Example	Chronology	Result	Difference	Addition	Conclusion
for example	first	as a result	however	furthermore	all in all
for instance	second	consequently	in contrast	in addition	in conclusion
	after that	therefore	on the other hand	moreover	in short
	later on				in summary
	next				
	then				

Using Commas with Transitions

The use of the comma is different with transitions than it is with coordinating conjunctions (see Chapter 1). Many transitions can go at the beginning, in the middle, or at the end of a sentence. No matter where they are, they are set off from the rest of the sentence by commas.

➤ For example, male cardinals are bright red.

OR

➤ Male cardinals, for example, are bright red.

OR

➤ Male cardinals are bright red, for example.

If the transition is a short, single-syllable transition and it comes at the beginning of a sentence, you don't have to use a comma.

➤ First, we went to the zoo.

OR

➤ First we went to the zoo.

Using *for example* and *such as*

The use of *for example* and *such as* can be confusing. *For example* is a transition, so a complete sentence (with a subject and a verb) must follow it. Use *such as*, preceded by a comma, if your example is a list of words and phrases.

➤ There are many ways animals can protect themselves from predators. *For example*, they can camouflage themselves, run fast, or fight.

OR

➤ There are many ways animals can protect themselves from predators, such as camouflage, running fast, or fighting.

■ PRACTICE 4: Combining Sentences Using Transitions

Connect the pairs of sentences by using one of the transitions in the chart on page 58. Vary the position of the transition. Then compare your sentences with a classmate.

1. The Pacific Ocean has many forms of life. There are fish, plants, and microscopic organisms.

   _____

2. The fox first found a perfect place to make a den. It started looking for a mate.

   _____

3. December is a winter month in the northern hemisphere. December is a summer month in the southern hemisphere.

   _____

4. The volcano erupted for ten days. The animals living in nearby habitats were killed.

   _____

5. If you want to enjoy a photographic safari, you need to have a lot of money. You need to tolerate difficult traveling.

   _____

Using Semicolons with Transitions

Transitions are usually followed by a comma when they occur at the beginning of a sentence. The usual pattern is:

Independent clause. *Transition*, independent clause.

> ➤ Some insects have weak defenses. *Therefore*, they camouflage themselves to look like predators.

Another common pattern is to use a semicolon instead of a period. By using this pattern, you are showing a stronger connection between the two independent clauses. In this case, the pattern is:

Independent clause; *transition*, independent clause.

> ➤ Some insects have weak defenses; *therefore*, they camouflage themselves to look like predators.

Here are a few examples of this pattern.

> ➤ Your first reason is clear; however, your second is unclear.

> ➤ It is raining today; therefore, my pet snake can't go outside.

> ➤ She finally saw the lioness; then, she quietly moved closer.

■ PRACTICE 5: Punctuating with Commas and Semicolons

Punctuate these sentences. Use commas and semicolons in the appropriate places.

1. Baby whales stay with their mothers for one to two years after that they usually go out on their own.

2. Loggers in the Northwest cut down the forests consequently they destroy some animals' natural habitats.

3. First we'll feed the dogs later on we'll feed ourselves.

4. The city government is trying many ways to decrease the number of wild cats in the park animal control officers are catching the cats and neutering them for instance.

5. Furthermore the police can suspend your dog's license.

6. Frank seems to hate people on the other hand he is very loving with his cats.

7. Some birds live permanently in the Arctic however most migrate.

8. I never leave home without my dogs for example.

IV WRITING TO COMMUNICATE

Your Turn

Plants and animals must adapt to a new ecosystem if they are to survive. Obviously, people are animals, too, but they are more able to make an adjustment to a new "habitat." You may have moved from the countryside to a city, from one state or region to another, or even to a different country and had to adapt to your new environment. Think of a specific move you made in the past. What adjustments did you have to make when you moved?

On the following page are the introductory and concluding paragraphs of an essay called "Adapting to a New Environment." Your assignment is to write three body paragraphs for this essay. Be sure to follow the process of writing discussed in Chapter 3.

Step 1: Analyzing the Assignment

Be sure that you have the answers to the following questions: *what, why, where, how,* and *when.*

Step 2: Brainstorming

Talk with a small group about how all of you have made changes in your lives as a result of moving to a different environment. You may have had to adapt in terms of:

● climate

● food

● shelter

- safety

- freedom of movement

What other adjustments can you think of?

Step 3: Organizing Your Ideas

Select three types of adaptations that you have had to make. Each adaptation will become a body paragraph in your essay.

Next, write a topic sentence for each paragraph, and write a few examples in note form underneath each topic sentence.

Step 4: Writing the First Draft

Write your body paragraphs. Use good paragraph format.

Step 5: Rewriting the First Draft

Reread your body paragraphs to make sure that each one supports the thesis statement. Make any necessary changes.

Share your essay with a classmate, using the Peer Help Worksheet on page 63 to help improve each other's essays.

Step 6: Writing the Final Paper (or Next Draft)

Taking the changes that you made to your second draft, write a final draft. Be sure to use good essay format, which includes a title.

Adapting to a New Environment

I. Introductory paragraph

➤ Human beings are very adaptable. We can live in most climates of the world. In the past, people tended to stay in the place they were born, but now we move easily from countryside to city, from one part of a country to another, and even from country to country. Each place has its own customs and ways of life, and countries also have different languages. *When I moved from _____ to _____ , I had to make several adjustments to my life.*

Note: You may not need to use two major supports for every paragraph, and you may want to have more than two in other paragraphs. As the writer, you make these decisions based on what you want to say to your readers.

II. Body

    A. Paragraph 1

➤ *Topic sentence:* _____

        Major support 1

➤ _____

            Minor support(s)

➤ _____

(continued)

Major support 2

➤ _____

    Minor support(s)

    ➤ _____

➤ *Concluding sentence:* _____

    _____

B. Paragraph 2

➤ *Topic sentence:* _____

    Major support 1

    ➤ _____

        Minor support(s)

        ➤ _____

    Major support 2

    ➤ _____

        Minor support(s)

        ➤ _____

➤ *Concluding sentence:* _____

    _____

C. Paragraph 3

➤ *Topic sentence:* _____

    Major support 1

    ➤ _____

        Minor support(s)

        ➤ _____

    Major support 2

    ➤ _____

        Minor support(s)

        ➤ _____

➤ *Concluding sentence:* _____

    _____

III. Concluding paragraph

➤ In conclusion, I wonder sometimes if I am the same person I was before I moved. By adjusting my _____, my _____, and my _____, I may appear to others as if I am a new person. However, I think of it not as having changed but as having grown.

Peer Help Worksheet

Trade essays and textbooks with a classmate. Read your classmate's essay while your classmate reads yours. Check off (✔) the items in your partner's book as you evaluate them. Then return the essays and books. If any of the items in your book are not checked off, and you agree with your partner, correct your essay before turning it in. Use a pencil if you write on your classmate's essay or book.

CONTENT

Which change in your partner's essay do you think was explained most clearly? Why?

ORGANIZATION

1 Does each body paragraph have a topic sentence? . . . . ❑

If *yes*, circle the topics and underline the controlling ideas.

If *no*, make a suggestion for an appropriate topic sentence.

2 Does each paragraph have sufficient support, in your view? . . . . ❑

If not, explain why to the writer.

3 Does each paragraph have a concluding sentence? . . . . ❑

If not, make a suggestion for an appropriate concluding sentence.

MECHANICS

1 Has each paragraph been indented? . . . . ❑

2 How many transitions are used in the essay?_____

Circle them in the essay.

3 Do you think that commas, semicolons, and periods are used correctly with transitions? . . . . ❑

If not, discuss any possible mistakes with the writer.

Writing to Communicate . . . More

Below are three further possible topics for essays about the themes of ecosystems, adaptation, and change. For help with the writing process, see Appendix 1 on page 173.

1. Are you familiar with any wild animals? Write an essay describing how certain animals in your native country adapt themselves and fit into their environment.

2. What were the major changes for you as you grew from a child to an adult? How did you adapt yourself?

3. Is the school you go to now different from the one you attended before? Write an essay about these changes and how you learned to adapt.

THE THESIS STATEMENT

The Five Senses

I VOCABULARY BUILDER

Most people agree that there are (at least) five ways that people perceive the world around them. The organs that perceive are the eyes, the ears, the tongue, the nose, and the skin. Read the information related to each of these organs.

Eyes

- Their sense is called *sight*.
- Your vision may be *fuzzy*, *clear*, or *20/20*, or you may be *blind*.
- Something may look *beautiful*, *adorable*, *pleasant*, or *ugly*.

Ears

- Their sense is called *hearing*.
- Your hearing may be *keen* or *dull*, or you may be *hard-of-hearing* or *deaf*.
- Something may sound *soothing*, *soft*, *loud*, or *noisy*.

Tongue

- Its sense is called *taste*.
- Something may taste *delicious*, *sweet*, *salty*, *sour*, or *bitter*.

Nose

- Its sense is called *smell*.

- Something may smell *sweet*, *spicy*, *sour*, or *pungent*.

Skin

- Its sense is called *touch*.

- Something may feel *firm*, *soft*, *gentle*, *hot*, or *cold*.

Now, imagine that you are in the place where these pictures were taken. Then list the adjectives that describe your reactions in terms of your senses. You can use the adjectives above or others you think of. If no adjectives are appropriate, write Ø.

Sight: _____

Hearing: _____

Taste: _____

Smell: _____

Touch: _____

Sight: _____

Hearing: _____

Taste: _____

Smell: _____

Touch: _____

Sight: _____

Hearing: _____

Taste: _____

Smell: _____

Touch: _____

What about you?

Which of your senses is the keenest? Tell your classmate why you think so.

Sight: _____

Hearing: _____

Taste: _____

Smell: _____

Touch: _____

The Thesis Statement

The **thesis statement** is the most important sentence in your essay because it contains the main idea for the whole essay. Just as major supporting sentences need to directly support the topic sentence in a paragraph, the body paragraphs in an essay must support the thesis statement in an essay.

■ **PRACTICE 1:** Analyzing the Thesis Statement in an Essay

Read the following essay. Underline the thesis statement. Then underline the topic sentences in each body paragraph. Discuss with a classmate how each body paragraph supports the thesis statement.

The Smell of Home

Last week a friend told me that she was reading a French novel in her university literature class. It was called *Remembrance of Things Past* and was written by Marcel Proust. She told me that in that book, a man bites into a little cookie called a madeleine and that the taste of the cookie makes him think about the past. For me, it is the sense of smell rather than the sense of taste that brings back happy memories.

The aroma of pipe tobacco always makes me smile. I know most people feel very differently about the smell of tobacco, but I like it for a simple reason: My grandfather used to smoke a pipe, and I adored my grandfather. After an especially good dinner, he used to settle into his favorite chair and go through a long ritual[1] of filling his pipe with something that looked like dead leaves and smelled of apples. Then he would light the pipe, lean back, and smile. The grandchildren gathered around him while he smoked and told us stories about when he was young and traveled the world on sailing ships. I felt safe and loved sitting near my grandfather while he smoked his pipe.

Another wonderful smell is the scent[2] of sweet rolls just coming out of the oven. When I was a child, my mother used to bake sweet rolls every Saturday. The children helped mix the dough with sugar and cinnamon[3] and shape it into little balls. Then we eagerly watched the timer as it counted down the minutes until the rolls were done. After my mother took out the hot rolls and placed them on the counter, the children mixed water and sugar into a paste.[4] When the rolls were cool, we spread the paste over the rolls. What a wonderful aroma! My mother let us eat one right away. We were very happy and secure there in the family kitchen with the smell of sweet, hot rolls.

My favorite aunt always wore a perfume that smelled like roses. My aunt was a tall and large woman who had lots of blond hair and wore flowered dresses. Her perfume was just like her: soft, friendly, warm, and cheerful. She had a lovely singing voice, and when I spent the night at my cousins' house, she would sit in the bedroom as we fell asleep singing old lullabies[5] in her rich, low voice. I fell asleep under the blankets to the smell of her rose perfume and her soft songs, feeling cared for and content.

These are just three examples of smells that I associate with happiness and safety. I don't know anyone who smokes a pipe these days, so I rarely smell pipe tobacco. However, I have my mother's recipe for sweet rolls, and I sometimes bake them for my friends. I like to wear more than one kind of perfume, but whenever I wear my rose perfume, I think of my aunt. Smells bring back wonderful memories.

[1]**ritual** *n.* something you do exactly the same way every time

[2]**scent** *n.* smell, aroma, odor

[3]**cinnamon** *n.* a spice often used in sweet things like cakes and cookies

[4]**paste** *n.* a mixture that is half liquid and half solid

[5]**lullaby** *n.* traditional songs that mothers sing to their babies

Parts of a Thesis Statement

Topic and Controlling Idea

Being able to write a clear thesis statement is essential for good essay writing in English. Like a topic sentence, a thesis statement has two main parts: a **topic** and a **controlling idea**. The topic is the subject of the essay, or what the essay is about. The controlling idea is what you are going to say about the topic.

As with topic sentences, it is not enough to just state the topic of the essay in the thesis statement. You must also tell the reader what your essay will say about the topic, which means that you need to have a controlling idea. Naturally, for any one topic there are many possibilities for controlling ideas. For example, with the topic *the sense of smell,* the thesis statement in the essay on page 66 has the underlined controlling idea:

➤ For me, it is the sense of smell rather than the sense of taste that <u>brings back happy memories</u>.

However, there could be other controlling ideas with the topic *the sense of smell* as shown in these examples.

➤ The sense of smell is <u>much stronger in dogs than it is in humans</u>.

In an essay with this thesis statement, you would support the controlling idea by giving examples of how dogs can smell better than people can.

➤ Many scientists believe that the sense of smell is <u>the most basic of all the senses in humans</u>.

In this essay, you would discuss how the sense of smell is more basic than the other senses.

The Predictor

Some thesis statements may also have a third component called a **predictor**. The predictor of a thesis statement can tell the reader how many body paragraphs there will be in the essay and/or what their content will be. For example:

➤ Blindness requires a heightened development of the other senses, especially touch and hearing.

In this thesis statement, the topic is *blindness*. The controlling idea is that it requires a *heightened development of the other senses*. The third part of this thesis statement lists the two senses that the author intends to discuss: *touch* and *hearing*. This is called the predictor because it predicts the number and content of the essay paragraphs. In this case, there will be two body paragraphs, one about the sense of touch and the other about the sense of hearing.

Look at these thesis statements. The topics of the statements are circled, the controlling ideas are underlined, and the predictors are boxed.

➤ The movie was a joy to watch because of its visual effects, surround sound, and actors.

➤ The deafening noise, the strong smells, and the ugly sights are the three main disadvantages to living in a large city.

■ PRACTICE 2: Identifying the Parts of Thesis Statements

Read these four thesis statements and answer the questions.

1. Although vision is important, many people manage very well without sight.
   What is the topic? _____
   What is the controlling idea? _____
   If there is a predictor, what is it? _____

2. Modern research suggests that the skin feels three main sensations: pressure, heat, and pain.
   What is the topic? _____
   What is the controlling idea? _____
   If there is a predictor, what is it? _____

3. My neighbor's dog is both blind and deaf, but he makes up for this in amazing ways.
   What is the topic? _____
   What is the controlling idea? _____
   If there is a predictor, what is it? _____

4. Losing the sense of taste can cause difficulties in a person's social, professional, and family life.
   What is the topic? _____
   What is the controlling idea? _____
   If there is a predictor, what is it? _____

Predict the content of the body paragraphs from these three thesis statements. Write two or three key words describing the content of the body paragraphs that you think will follow each thesis statement.

1. Pitch, rhythm, and melody form the main elements of music.

   Body paragraph 1: _____*pitch*_____

   Body paragraph 2: _____

   Body paragraph 3: _____

2. There are many aids for people to improve their vision, such as corrective lenses, eye training, and surgery.

   Body paragraph 1: _____

   Body paragraph 2: _____

   Body paragraph 3: _____

3. Seasickness, which happens when you have an imbalance in the inner ears, can be prevented by a few simple methods.

   Body paragraph 1: _____

   Body paragraph 2: _____

   Body paragraph 3: _____

More on Thesis Statements

In addition to a topic, controlling idea, and predictor, there are other characteristics that thesis statements must have:

1. A thesis statement must be a *statement,* not a question.

Not a thesis statement:	Is kimchi an acquired taste?
Thesis statement:	Kimchi is an acquired taste.

2. A thesis statement must be a *complete sentence.* This means that it must have a subject and a verb with a tense.

Not a thesis statement:	Music: the food of love.
Thesis statement:	Music is the food of love.

3. A thesis statement is an *opinion* or shows *intent*; it cannot be a simple statement of fact. A fact does not need any support, and therefore you cannot write an essay about it.

Not a thesis statement:	Dogs have a sense of smell.
Thesis statement:	Dogs use their keen sense of smell in many ways.

4. A thesis statement must *state* the controlling idea. This means that you must state your position on the topic; you cannot simply announce the topic of your essay.

Not a thesis statement:	This essay is about Helen Keller.
Thesis statement:	Both blind and deaf, Helen Keller learned to communicate through touch alone.

Helen Keller

5. A thesis statement should have only *one* controlling idea.

| *Not a thesis statement:* | My cousin has an excellent sense of pitch, and she is also a famous dancer. |
| *Thesis statement:* | My cousin's excellent sense of pitch has made her an accomplished musician. |

■ **PRACTICE 4:** **Evaluating Thesis Statements**

Put a check mark (✓) in front of the sentences that are thesis statements. If a sentence is not a thesis statement, write the number(s) of the rule(s) (1–5, above) it breaks on the line in front of it, and then change it to make a thesis statement. For example:

___4___   I'm going to write about foods that have special meaning for my family.
Kimchi and moon cakes are two foods that have special meaning for my family.

_____ 1. Hearing is more important than sight.

_____

_____ 2. My mother wears contact lenses.

_____

_____ 3. This essay is about how different people react to heat.

_____

_____ 4. Why do people react differently to heat?

_____

_____ 5. In the past, a keen sense of hearing was crucial to survival.

_____

_____ 6. I prefer music with a rapid tempo, but I also like blues.

_____

_____ 7. There are advantages and disadvantages to having a sharp sense of smell.

_____

_____ 8. There are more advantages than disadvantages to having a sharp sense of smell.

_____

_____ 9. The sense of smell: an analysis.

_____

_____ 10. In this essay, I will describe the feelings that the scent of my mother's cooking gives me.

_____

■ **PRACTICE 5:** **Writing Thesis Statements**

Choose five of these eight topics and write a good thesis statement for each. At least three of your five statements should have a predictor. Then exchange papers with a classmate. Evaluate each other's thesis statements by circling the topics, underlining the controlling ideas, and putting a box around the predictors.

➤ (Chocolate) is *pleasing to three of my senses:* sight, smell, and taste .

1. Food
2. Sounds of home
3. Noise pollution
4. Living in the city

5. Beauty
6. My favorite smells
7. My grandfather's touch
8. Animals' senses

III STRUCTURE AND MECHANICS

Prepositional Phrases

Writing Prepositional Phrases

A **prepositional phrase** consists of a preposition and its object, which is always a noun. Nouns can be single words, phrases, or gerunds.

➤ **Unlike** *mangoes,* apples can be bought all year long.

➤ Blind people use their fingers to read **instead of** *their eyes.*

➤ **In addition to** *baking,* Juanita also enjoys tasting.

There are countless prepositions in English, but the following charts have some common ones.

Chronology	Location	Causation	Unexpected Result
after before during prior to since until	above behind below in front of next to on top of to the left of to the right of under	because of due to	despite in spite of

Contrast	Direct Contrast	Similarity	Addition
different from in contrast to instead of	unlike	like similar to	in addition to

Prepositional Phrases and Commas

In Chapter 3, you learned about adverb clauses and their punctuation patterns. As a review, look at these examples.

If the adverb clause comes *before* the independent clause, use a comma.

➤ After it was discovered that chocolate is good for your heart, the sales of chocolate bars increased.

If the adverb clause comes *after* the independent clause, don't use a comma.

➤ The sales of chocolate bars increased after it was discovered that chocolate is good for your heart.

The punctuation pattern for prepositional phrases is the same. If the prepositional phrase comes at the beginning of a clause, use a comma. If it comes at the end, don't use a comma. For example:

➤ *Despite the calories,* I can't resist chocolate.

➤ I can't resist chocolate *despite the calories.*

■ PRACTICE 6: Using Commas with Prepositional Phrases

Underline the prepositional phrases in the following sentences. Then insert a comma in the sentence if necessary.

1. Like everyone in my family my mother tastes food while she's cooking it.
2. Above the house you could see a big balloon carrying two people.
3. Min Hee resisted opening the oven in spite of the wonderful smell in the kitchen.
4. In addition to reading lips deaf people also communicate through sign language.
5. Let's listen to rock and roll music instead of country and western.
6. Unlike Olivia Chris looks just like her mother.
7. We decided to postpone seeing the movie until Friday.
8. Because of her short height Jane couldn't see the package on top of the shelf.

IV WRITING TO COMMUNICATE

Your Turn

In this section, you will brainstorm, organize your ideas, and write the body paragraphs for one of the thesis statements you wrote for Practice 5 on page 71.

Brainstorming

In Chapter 3 on pages 33–35, you learned some common ways of brainstorming: using a mind map, using columns, and freewriting. Use one of these techniques to generate ideas about your thesis statement.

Organizing Your Ideas

Try to make three groupings of the ideas you brainstormed. You will probably eliminate some ideas and add others. Then use this outline to organize your ideas. Write your topic sentences for the body paragraphs and the major supporting points that you want to use. You may also want to fill in the minor supporting points as you think of them.

Body paragraph 1

➤ *Topic sentence:* _____

_____

Major support

➤ _____

Minor support(s)

➤ _____

Major support

➤ _____

Minor support(s)

➤ _____

➤ *Concluding sentence:* _____

_____

Body paragraph 2 _____

➤ *Topic sentence:* _____

_____

Major support

➤ _____

Minor support(s)

➤ _____

Major support

➤ _____

Minor support(s)

➤ _____

➤ *Concluding sentence:* _____

_____

(continued)

Body paragraph 3 _____

➤ *Topic sentence:* _____

Major support

➤ _____

   Minor support(s)

   ➤ _____

Major support

➤ _____

   Minor support(s)

   ➤ _____

➤ *Concluding sentence:* _____

_____

Writing a First Draft

Now write the first draft of your essay. Write your thesis statement as a separate one-sentence paragraph and add two or three body paragraphs, following your outline. Give your essay a title. Be sure to use correct paragraph format. (Note that this essay will not be a complete essay because it does not have an introductory paragraph and a concluding paragraph. These types of paragraphs will be discussed in the next two chapters.)

Peer Help Worksheet

Trade essays and textbooks with a classmate. Read your classmate's essay while your classmate reads yours. Check off (✔) the items in your partner's book as you evaluate them. Then return the essays and books. If any of the items in your book are not checked off, and you agree with your partner, correct your essay before turning it in. Use a pencil if you write on your classmate's essay or book.

CONTENT

1 What did you learn from your partner's essay?

2 Does each body paragraph support the thesis statement? . . . . . ❑

3 Is each paragraph unified?. . . . . ❑

4 Underline (in pencil) any sentences that you think are irrelevant.

ORGANIZATION

1 Does each body paragraph have a topic sentence?. . . . . ❑

2 Does each body paragraph have coherence and cohesion? . . . . ❑

3 Does each body paragraph have a concluding sentence? . . . . . . ❑

MECHANICS

1 Is the thesis statement indented? . . . . ❑

2 Do you think commas are used correctly with adverb clauses
and prepositional phrases? . . . . ❑

If not, discuss any possible mistakes with the writer.

Writing to Communicate . . . More

For extra writing practice, write another thesis statement and support it with two or three body paragraphs. Use the topic suggested here:

➤ Sensory perceptions strongly influence memories. The smell of a certain soap, the taste of a peanut butter cookie, or the touch of a wool sweater you had when you were a child can make you remember things you thought you had forgotten.

Choose one such sensory perception and describe the memories that it gives you. For example, your thesis statement could be:

➤ The sounds of _____ , _____ , and _____ remind me of my childhood home.

➤ The taste of _____ reminds me of my favorite holidays.

➤ The smell of _____ , the sound of _____ , and the sight of _____ remind me of my father.

In the body of your essay, write two or three paragraphs to support your thesis statement. For further help with the writing process, see Appendix 1 on page 173.

Nature vs. Nurture

I VOCABULARY BUILDER

Some people think that we are born with our personalities, just as we are born with the physical traits that our parents pass on to us. They believe that *nature* makes us who we are. Other people think that the way we are raised and the environment in which we live shape our personalities. We call this *nurture*. Which do you think is more important in forming our personalities: nature or nurture?

Study the words for Nature *and* Nurture *with a classmate. Then use them to complete the paragraph on page 77.*

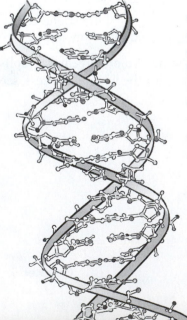

Nature

gene *n.* a part of a cell in a living thing that controls how it develops
genetic *adj.* relating to genes or genetics
heredity *n.* the process of passing on a physical quality from a parent to a child
innate *adj.* a quality that has been part of your nature since you were born
tendency *n.* if someone has a tendency to do something, he or she is likely to do it

Nurture

atmosphere *n.* the mood of an event, situation, or place

circumstance *n.* the facts or conditions that affect a situation, action, or event

culture *n.* the art, beliefs, behavior, and ideas of a particular society

environment *n.* the situation, things, and people that affect you

influence *v.* to have an effect on the way someone or something develops, behaves, or thinks

What about you?

What made you who you are? Genetics? Environment? Share your thoughts with a classmate.

Making Me Who I Am

Both my ____environment____ and my ____genes____ have shaped the way I am. The _____ of my native country places a lot of importance on respectful behavior, so this has certainly helped make me a quiet, respectful person. In addition, the _____ in our house was always calm. Nobody shouted. This gave me a relaxed attitude toward life. On the other hand, I'm sure the _____ inheritance from my ancestors has shaped me, too. All four of my grandparents had _____ abilities in the arts. I'm not a good artist, but I do have a _____ to surround myself with music and beautiful things.

All in all, I feel that both the nurture my parents gave me while I was growing up and my inborn nature have played a part in making me who I am.

Guidelines for Introductory Paragraphs

The first paragraph in an essay is called the **introductory paragraph**. There are two purposes of the introductory paragraph: to get the readers' attention and to introduce them to the subject of your essay. In other words, you need to lead readers to the subject of the essay in an interesting way and convince them that reading your essay will be worth their time.

There are several guidelines for writing a good introductory paragraph.

- It must be relevant to the topic; that is, it should not introduce material not covered in the essay.

- It should not give detailed information about the main ideas of the essay. Detailed information belongs in the body paragraphs.

- There should be at least two sentences before the thesis statement.

- The thesis statement should come at the end of the introductory paragraph.

Types of Introductory Paragraphs

There are many ways for a writer to get the readers' attention in an introductory paragraph. Three of the most common ways are discussed here. In your essays, try to develop the skill of writing different types of introductions, so your essays do not become too predictable.

General to Specific

This is perhaps the most common type of introduction. It begins with a general statement of the larger topic, and then each sentence narrows it down until you get to the specific thesis statement.

Anecdote

An anecdote is a brief story that illustrates your topic. In a personal anecdote, you tell a story about your own experiences that are relevant to the thesis. In a third-person anecdote, you tell a story about someone else. You can base your story on a real person(s), or you can make up a story.

Historical

You may also choose to write a brief historical introduction to your essay. Since this is just the introduction to the essay, you don't need to give a detailed historical account, just an overview.

■ **PRACTICE 1: Identifying Types of Introductory Paragraphs**

The same thesis statement is introduced four different ways in the following models. Identify the type of introductory paragraph in each. Use these labels:

GS for General to Specific
A for Anecdote
H for Historical

Paragraph 1: _____

Throughout my childhood, I was always in trouble at school. The teachers said I was an "underachiever" and "lazy." I had a hard time learning to read. When I was fourteen years old, my parents finally realized what was wrong: I am dyslexic.[1] They got me the extra help I needed, and now I am the owner of a chain of grocery stores, I have a loving family and two children, and I was recently elected mayor of our town. In my opinion, *success depends more on hard work than on innate ability*.

[1]**dyslexic** *adj.* referring to a person who has the learning disability dyslexia, which causes difficulty with reading and writing

Paragraph 2: _____

With the exception of Native Americans, the United States is a country of immigrants. Each new group of immigrants arrived bringing their hopes, their dreams, and their work ethic,[1] and they all had to start at the bottom. One by one, the immigrant groups, such as the Irish, the Italians, the Chinese, the Vietnamese, and the Latinos, struggled for acceptance and respect. Each group faced enormous obstacles[2] from discrimination. In the end, however, each succeeded and now makes up an important part of this country. As immigrants' experiences have shown, *success depends more on hard work than on innate ability*.

[1]**work ethic** *n.* the belief that hard work is the way to succeed

[2]**obstacle** *n.* something that makes it difficult to succeed

Paragraph 3: _____

Some people seem to learn languages almost without effort. My cousin Liz, on the other hand, struggled with Italian all through high school. She never gave up, however. After high school, she had a chance to become a flight attendant, but one job requirement was that she had to speak a foreign language. In her determination, she borrowed money from her parents and went to Italy for a year to study at a language school. She says it was the hardest thing she had ever done, but she did it. In fact, when I visited her in Rome last year, she had become completely fluent, had a great job with Alitalia, the Italian airline, and loved her life. Liz's story shows that *success depends more on hard work than on innate ability*.

What about you?

"Success is 10 percent inspiration and 90 percent perspiration" is a common proverb. How would you interpret this proverb? Share your thoughts with your classmate.

Paragraph 4: _____

All human beings want to feel successful, but we are not born with the same abilities. However, we all have the ability to learn. By working hard at learning something, all of us can master it to a certain extent. Even the most famous artists say that practice is more important than their native talent. *Success depends more on hard work than on innate ability.*

■ **PRACTICE 2:** **Evaluating Introductory Paragraphs**

Read the four introductory paragraphs that follow. Check off (✓) the features of a good introduction that they have (remember, they must have all four to be a good introduction).

1. Some people have a happy life and some people don't. My friend Tony has a miserable life. He just got divorced, and now his wife won't let him see his children. To live a happy life, a good environment is more important than good genes.

   ❑ It is relevant to the topic of the essay.

   ❑ It contains at least three sentences.

   ❑ It doesn't give details that belong in the body of the essay.

   ❑ It ends with the thesis statement.

2. First, a good environment can make you healthier, which can make you happy. Second, if you live in a good environment, you probably have many friends who can help you when you need it. Friends are important for emotional health as well. People with friends are happier than people without friends. Also, a good environment is probably safer, so you don't have to be afraid to walk down the street. Being safe makes everyone happy. To live a happy life, a good environment is more important than good genes.

☐ It is relevant to the topic of the essay.

☐ It contains at least three sentences.

☐ It doesn't give details that belong in the body of the essay.

☐ It ends with the thesis statement.

3. It is said that your mother and father make you what you are. You get your genes from them, and they may have great genes. However, if they don't raise you in a safe, loving environment, you may never be happy. To live a happy life, a good environment is more important than good genes.

☐ It is relevant to the topic of the essay.

☐ It contains at least three sentences.

☐ It doesn't give details that belong in the body of the essay.

☐ It ends with the thesis statement.

4. Before the nineteenth century, most people lived in dirty, smelly, unhealthy environments. To live a happy life, a good environment is more important than good genes.

☐ It is relevant to the topic of the essay.

☐ It contains at least three sentences.

☐ It doesn't give details that belong in the body of the essay.

☐ It ends with the thesis statement.

5. Environment is much more important that genes when you are growing up. A good example of this is the millions of people in the world who were born with physical challenges. If people are raised in a good environment, they can be successful and live a happy life.

☐ It is relevant to the topic of the essay.

☐ It contains at least three sentences.

☐ It doesn't give details that belong in the body of the essay.

☐ It ends with the thesis statement.

Choose one of the thesis statements below. Then write at least two introductory paragraphs for it. Remember that you can introduce a thesis statement by using anecdotes (personal or third person), by briefly providing historical information, or by going from general ideas to specific ones.

1. The influence of my mother and father has made me who I am today.
2. A good environment for children must have three characteristics.
3. The study of genetics can be dangerous.

III STRUCTURE AND MECHANICS

Avoiding Fragments

As you learned in Chapter 1, the minimum sentence in written English consists of a subject and a verb; this is called an **independent clause**. (The only exception to this rule is an imperative sentence. In the case of an imperative, such as *Sit down!,* the sentence has the "hidden subject," *you*.) Strings of words that either do not have a subject or do not have a verb are called **fragments** and must be corrected. Another kind of fragment is a dependent clause that is not connected to an independent clause. Look at these fragments:

➤ Because I wanted a safer neighborhood.

➤ John singing in the shower.

➤ Dancing and laughing at the party downtown.

➤ For example, a big backyard.

Fragments should never be used in academic writing, but there are many ways to correct them once you have found them. Read how the fragments above were corrected.

1. *Because I wanted a safer neighborhood* is a dependent clause. A dependent clause must be connected to an independent clause. You, the writer, must decide whether it should be connected to the sentence before it or after it. Possible corrections are:

   ➤ **Because I wanted a safer neighborhood,** I started looking for a new home.

   OR

   ➤ I started looking for a new home **because I wanted a safer neighborhood.**

2. In *John singing in the shower, singing* is a form of a verb, but it does not have a tense. There are three forms of a verb in English that do not have a tense: the present participle (*singing*), the past participle (*sung*), and the infinitive (*to sing*). *Singing* is the present participle of the verb *sing*. To make this fragment into a sentence, you need to change the present participle to a verb with a tense. Possible corrections are:

> John was singing in the shower.

OR

> John sings in the shower (every morning).

3. *Dancing and laughing at the party downtown* is a fragment because it does not have a subject. In addition, the verbs are present participles. Possible corrections are:

> We were dancing and laughing at the party downtown.

OR

> Dancing and laughing at the party downtown, we exhausted ourselves.

4. *For example, a big backyard* has only a noun phrase (*a big backyard*) and no verb. You need to add a verb and to decide if the noun phrase is the subject or object of the sentence. Possible corrections are:

> For example, a big backyard is great for growing vegetables.

OR

> For example, I wanted a big backyard.

■ **PRACTICE 4: Identifying Fragments**

This paragraph has four fragments. Find them and correct them.

Nature First

In my opinion. Heredity plays a more important role in a child's personality development than environment does. First, adopted twins. When these twins, who were separated at birth, are reunited in adulthood, they find many likes and dislikes in common. Second, when adopted children are reunited with their biological parents. They often find many similar personality attributes. Indicating that genes are as important in a child's development as the environment.

Your Turn

This essay about the causes of violence in U.S. society does not have an introductory paragraph. First, read the essay and underline the topic sentences. Then write an appropriate introductory paragraph with a good thesis statement.

Violence: Nature or Nurture?

_____

_____

_____

_____

_____

First of all, it's obvious that people become violent when they are trying to protect someone or something. A clear example of this is when gang members want to protect their neighborhoods from the "invasion" of members of other gangs. However, even people who have never shown any violent tendencies might also commit a violent crime if a loved one is in danger. It is not in their nature to commit violence, but the circumstances (or environment) cause the violence. In short, when a situation is threatening, not only gang members but also average people can act violently.

It's clear, too, that in an environment where guns are readily available, more violent crimes are committed. When you compare the United States to any country that does not allow its citizens to own guns, you will see that this is true. In a volatile[1] situation, it's easier to reach for the gun than to continue arguing. Again, this type of environment leads to violence in people not prone[2] to violence; that is, the tendency to violence doesn't come from the genes that a person has.

Most importantly, some people have been raised without a sense of respect for other people. They place little value on a human life. Indeed, you sometimes hear today that some children want to hurt someone just to know what it feels like. This is also environmental. Parents and schools can teach children to respect other people. How children perceive other people's rights depends on the type of situation in which they are raised.

In short, I believe that people are not born violent. They are not born with genes that make them violent. It's the environment that they are born *into* and the situations that they find themselves in that cause them to become violent.

[1]**volatile** *adj.* quickly changing   [2]**prone** *adj.* likely to do something

Peer Help Worksheet

Trade introductory paragraphs and textbooks with a classmate. Read your classmate's paragraph while your classmate reads yours. Check off (✔) the items in your partner's book as you evaluate them. Then return the paragraphs and books. If any of the items in your book are not checked off, and you agree with your partner, correct your paragraph before turning it in. Use a pencil if you write on your classmate's paragraph or book.

CONTENT

1 What caught your attention in this introductory paragraph? What made it interesting to read?

2 What type of organization does the introductory paragraph follow? (Check one.)

  a. anecdote . . . . ❑

  b. historical . . . . ❑

  c. general to specific . . . . ❑

3 Is this introductory paragraph relevant to the thesis statement? . . . ❑

4 Does the introductory paragraph avoid giving details that belong in the body of the essay?. . . . . ❑

5 Are there at least two sentences before the thesis statement? . . . ❑

ORGANIZATION

1 Underline the thesis statement. Does it have a clear topic and controlling idea? . . . . ❑

2 Does the thesis statement have a predictor? . . . . ❑

3 Is the thesis statement at the end of the introductory paragraph? . . . . ❑

MECHANICS

Do you think there are any fragments in this paragaph? . . . . ❑

If so, point them out to your classmate.

Writing to Communicate . . . More

For more writing practice, write an introductory paragraph for one of these thesis statements.

1. **Write a historical introduction.**

   Genetics is an important field of study because we can learn which health factors we can influence and which ones we can't.

2. **Write a general-to-specific introduction.**

   We should stop studying genetics because it is an invasion of privacy and because the information can be misused by employers and insurance companies.

3. **Write an anecdotal introduction.**

   It's not my lifestyle that makes me thin;* it's my genes.

   *You can use another adjective if you like.

CHAPTER 7

THE CONCLUDING PARAGRAPH

The State of the Earth

I VOCABULARY BUILDER

A. Look at the words in the box below. With a classmate, choose the correct word for each picture and write the words on the lines.

continents	garbage	satellite
endangered species	insect species	tornado

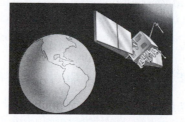

_____

_____

_____

_____

_____

_____

B. *With a classmate, try to match these numbers with their explanation. Then check your answers at the bottom of the page.*

1. 71   **a.** number of **insect species**

2. 3   **b.** number of **endangered species**

3. 5   **c.** percent of Earth's **surface** that is water

4. 7   **d.** tons of **garbage** the United States produces in a year

5. 75   **e.** number of weather **satellites**

6. 1,000+   **f.** number of **continents**

7. 900,000   **g.** percent of Earth's water that is **fresh**

8. 200,000,000   **h.** percent of worldwide **tornadoes** that occur in the United States

II WRITING FOCUS

Parts of a Concluding Paragraph

The last paragraph of your essay is, of course, the **concluding paragraph**. This paragraph has a very important function. Since it is the last paragraph to be read, you want your reader to leave with a clear understanding of your essay's point.

A concluding paragraph consists of a summary of the points made in your body paragraphs, a restatement of the thesis statement, and/or a final comment on your topic. You may choose one of these ways to end your essay, or you may choose two or three.

Finally, do not introduce new information about the topic of the essay. New information should go in another body paragraph, not in the concluding paragraph.

Summary Concluding Paragraphs

One way to end your essay is to summarize its main points. When you write these types of concluding paragraphs, you need to be sure that you include the main point of each body paragraph. Your conclusion won't be complete if you leave one point out.

■ PRACTICE 1: Analyzing a Concluding Paragraph

Find the main points in the following essay by underlining the topic sentence in each body paragraph. Then check the concluding paragraph. Are all the points mentioned?

Answers: 1. c 2. g 3. e 4. f 5. h 6. b 7. a 8. d

Stormy Weather

Most of us prefer sunshine and calm weather. We like sunbathing on a warm beach or hiking in the mountains on a clear, cloudless day. However, some people actually prefer intense storms. These people are ocean racers, storm spotters, and storm chasers, and they love the challenge of fighting nature and winning.

Ocean racers are people who prefer strong winds to a soft breeze. They need the strong winds to win a sailboat race. The crew[1] on an ocean racing sailboat uses all the latest technology to predict the wind direction and strength, and then they seek the location where the wind is the strongest. They are happiest when the mast[2] on the boat is almost horizontal.

The second group, storm spotters, consists of people who volunteer to help predict the weather for those who need accurate information, such as boat captains. Their job is to report the weather conditions they see and hear in their area. This is more accurate than radar or satellite information. Storm spotters can actually save lives by reporting dangerous weather to the weather service and local emergency agencies. These people in turn send the news out by radio. Storm spotters want to help out during severe[3] weather so that people will be safe.

Storm chasers make up the last group, and they are the real weather fanatics.[4] They follow storms in their cars or trucks. They do not get paid for this; in fact, they do it for fun. Chasers are usually looking for tornados, but they chase other severe weather as well. Their goal is to get a perfect photograph of a storm. You can say that storm chasers are the ultimate weather lovers.

In conclusion, there are three kinds of bad-weather lovers. One is the captain of an ocean racing sailboat, who chases stronger winds to win a race. Another is the volunteer storm spotter who provides invaluable information. The last is the fun-loving storm chaser who travels hundreds of miles to get the perfect photograph.

---

[1]**crew** *n.* all the people who work together on a ship or airplane

[2]**mast** *n.* a tall pole on which the sails of a ship are hung

[3]**severe** *adj.* very bad or serious

[4]**fanatic** *n.* someone who likes a particular thing or activity very much

Restatement Concluding Paragraphs

An alternative to a summary is a restatement of the idea of your thesis statement. Here is another concluding paragraph for the essay on weather.

Circle the words in this concluding paragraph that are synonyms for words in the thesis statement.

Model Paragraph 1

> In conclusion, when people say that they love the weather, they usually mean that they love sunny weather. Only people like the ocean racer, the storm spotter, and the storm chaser can say that they love the weather because they live to battle nature at its wildest.

Final Comment Concluding Paragraph

Often, a concluding paragraph is most effective when you add a final comment to a summary or a restatement. A final comment can make a concluding paragraph more personal. It can also invite readers to think about how the essay is directly related to their lives. Look at another alternative to the original concluding paragraph for the essay on weather.

Underline the parts of this concluding paragraph that connect the reader to the essay.

Model Paragraph 2

> **What about you?**
> What kinds of severe weather does your country have? Tell your classmate.

> In conclusion, the next time you walk outside and think that the weather is great, think about the people who prefer intense storms. Think about the ocean racing captain who tries to find the strongest winds, the storm spotter who is gathering information in wet and windy conditions, and the storm chaser who is crazy for storms. You might be glad that you can just sit back and enjoy the sunny weather.

■ PRACTICE 2: **Evaluating Concluding Paragraphs**

The following essay does not have a concluding paragraph. Read the essay and the three possible concluding paragraphs that follow. Choose the best one. Then explain your choice to a classmate.

The Small Strengths of Nature

We often think, and rightly so, that human beings are destroying the environment, but it is also true that sometimes the Earth and the environment become the destroyers. Earthquakes, hurricanes, and droughts[1] cause huge damage to the Earth. However, on a much smaller scale, nature is always demonstrating to us that it is stronger than we are.

For example, we cut down trees and construct houses, offices, apartment buildings, roads, and sidewalks. Then we plant other trees just where we want them so that our gardens will be perfect. Over the years, the trees slowly grow taller, their roots grow deeper, and suddenly, our nice roads and sidewalks get cracks in them. We think that we are strong, but those trees are stronger.

Furthermore, nature's insects are far stronger than any human being. They come into our nicely constructed environments and either destroy them or make them very unpleasant to live in. Termites[2] can totally destroy a house, and ants can spoil our food. Indeed, the cockroaches in our cupboard have ancestors that go back millions and millions of years. How can we possibly expect to control them? In short, it's clear that insects are stronger than humans.

Even on a microscopic level, the environment is more powerful than we are. Our bodies and our scientists have developed ways of fighting the many bacteria[3] and viruses[4] that cause serious diseases and death. Nevertheless, there is still no cure for the common cold. We may develop vaccines[5] and antibiotics[6] to protect us from many viruses and bacteria, but they can change. Then it becomes even harder to destroy them. In other words, they are often stronger than we are.

---

[1]**drought** *n.* a long period of dry weather when there is not enough water

[2]**termite** *n.* an insect that eats wood from trees and buildings

[3]**bacteria** *n.* very small living things that sometimes cause disease

[4]**virus** *n.* a very small living thing that causes infectious illnesses

[5]**vaccine** *n.* a substance that is used to protect people from disease, usually injected into the body

[6]**antibiotic** *n.* a drug that is used in order to kill bacteria and cure infections

Possible Concluding Paragraphs

a. In short, we live in a world that is stronger than we are. Trees will win any long-term battle over concrete, and termites can eat buildings. This means that we will not eventually kill the Earth.

b. In conclusion, I think these small examples of nature's being stronger than humans are comforting. While we try to control and thereby destroy our environment, the environment keeps renewing itself in small ways. Humans as a species may not survive, but I believe the Earth will.

c. All in all, nature is strong. In fact, it demonstrates this to us every day with its plants, insects, microscopic life, and weather. Isn't it time we pay attention to this fact and stop trying to control it?

What about you?

What are some other ways in which nature is stronger than human beings? Share your thoughts with a classmate.

Avoiding Run-on Sentences

In the last chapter, you learned about fragments and how to avoid them. Another common punctuation problem is the **run-on sentence**. In run-on sentences, two or more independent clauses follow each other without any punctuation. Look at this example of a run-on sentence:

➤ Following storms can be dangerous storm chasers run after them.

There are five common ways to correct run-on sentences:

1. Make two separate sentences.

   ➤ Following storms can be dangerous. **S**torm chasers run after them.

2. Add a coordinating conjunction (see Chapter 2).

   ➤ Following storms can be dangerous, **but** storm chasers run after them.

3. Add a subordinating conjunction (see Chapter 3).

   ➤ **Even though** following storms can be dangerous, storm chasers run after them.

   ➤ Storm chasers run after storms **even though** following storms can be dangerous.

4. Add a transition (see Chapter 4).

   ➤ Following storms can be dangerous. **Nevertheless,** storm chasers run after them.

   ➤ Following storms can be dangerous; **nevertheless,** storm chasers run after them.

5. Make one independent clause into a prepositional phrase (see Chapter 5).

   ➤ **Despite the danger,** storm chasers run after storms.

   ➤ Storm chasers run after storms **despite the danger.**

■ **PRACTICE 3:** Correcting Run-on Sentences

Correct each of the run-on sentences using the five different ways discussed above.

Item 1

Cockroaches will be around forever they are strong.

1. _____

2. _____

3. _____

4. _____

5. _____

(*Hint:* Use "because of" followed by the noun form of "strong.")

Item 2

Helene gets up she checks the weather.

1. _____
2. _____
3. _____
4. _____
5. _____

(*Hint*: Use "after" and the *-ing* form of "get.")

■ **PRACTICE 4:** **Finding and Correcting Run-on Sentences**

Find the three run-on sentences in the passage below. Then rewrite the passage so that the punctuation is correct. Use good paragraph format.

The Endangered Habitats of Whales

The habitats of many endangered whales are making it hard for them to live for example, many bodies of waters are polluted with chemicals and garbage. The chemicals make them sick, and the garbage makes it difficult for them to move. Another example is the noise of ships and construction projects that occur in the ocean the ability to hear is very important to whales. They use it to navigate, to communicate with each other, and to locate prey in short, whales are endangered by changes that we make to their living spaces.

IV WRITING TO COMMUNICATE

Your Turn

This essay does not have a concluding paragraph. As you read through the essay, underline the thesis statement and the topic sentences. Then, on a separate piece of paper, write two concluding paragraphs: one with a summary and a final comment, and the other with a restatement and a final comment.

Pollution: Looking Back and Going Ahead

As we begin a new century, it might be a good idea to look back and see where we've been. Human beings accomplished many advances in medicine, technology, and the quality of life in the twentieth century. However, we often made these advances at the expense of our Earth. As the century closed, we were beginning to make progress in preventing the pollution of our air, water, and land, but there is still a long way to go.

(continued)

In the United States, air pollution was at its worst in the 1960s. In some cities, fumes[1] from cars and factories made it difficult to breathe on a hot summer day. Then, in 1970, the Clean Air Act was passed by Congress, and the Environmental Protection Agency created safe standards for car and factory emissions.[2] Since then, the air quality in many American cities has become noticeably better. Other countries also established standards, and several international agreements were made. However, there are still too many cars on the road. In developing countries especially, it is difficult to choose to protect the environment when people need jobs, so factories continue to pollute the air.

Water pollution is also a serious concern. People cannot live without water, but over the years it has been polluted by chemicals from factories and oil spills.[3] Drinking or bathing in such polluted water causes illness or even death. In 1956, Congress passed laws to clean and protect our water. Nevertheless, too many people in the United States and other countries do not have clean drinking water. We must solve this problem in the twenty-first century if we hope to survive.

Land pollution was also a problem because of the millions of tons of garbage that people create every year. There are landfills,[4] but people are producing more garbage every year. The people of the United States and other developed nations (who create the majority of the garbage in the world) must solve this problem in this century. Many countries have begun strong recycling efforts, but it is only the beginning. The goal should be to recycle 100 percent of our garbage.

---

[1]**fume** *n.* strong-smelling gas or smoke that is unpleasant to breathe

[2]**emission** *n.* the gas that is sent out of cars and factories

[3]**oil spill** *n.* an amount of oil that is accidentally released into the ocean

[4]**landfill** *n.* a place where garbage is buried in large amounts

Peer Help Worksheet

Trade concluding paragraphs and textbooks with a classmate. Read your classmate's paragraphs while your classmate reads yours. Check off (✓) the items in your partner's book as you evaluate them. Then return the paragraphs and books. If any of the items in your book are not checked off, and you agree with your partner, correct your paragraphs before turning them in. Use a pencil if you write on your classmate's paragraphs or book.

CONTENT

Which of your partner's concluding paragraphs is the most effective, in your opinion? Why?

ORGANIZATION

1 Look at your partner's first paragraph.

a. Which of the three ways to conclude does it use? (Check all that apply.)

- Summary (Are all the points of the body paragraphs included?) . . . . ❑

- Restatement of the thesis statement (Circle the synonyms used.) . . . . ❑

- Final comment . . . . ❑

b. Is there any new information? If so, underline it.

2 Look at your partner's second paragraph.

a. Which of the three ways to conclude does it use? (Check all that apply.)

- Summary (Are all the points of the body paragraphs included?) . . . . ❑

- Restatement of the thesis statement (Circle the synonyms used.) . . . . ❑

- Final comment . . . . ❑

b. Is there any new information? If so, underline it.

MECHANICS

Do you think there are any run-on sentences in the paragraphs? . . . ❑

If so, suggest a correction to your classmate.

Writing to Communicate . . . More

For more practice writing concluding paragraphs, write one for this essay on a separate sheet of paper.

The Uniqueness of Antarctica

When most people think about going on vacation, they think about going to a tropical island where they can relax in the sun. Others think that camping in mountains and hiking through forests make the best vacations. I have a different idea. The best vacation I ever had was the eco-cruise[1] I took to Antarctica. Antarctica is unlike any other place in the world.

The first thing you notice is the beauty. Everything looks pure and untouched. The contrast between the ice and water is startling. The ice can be the whitest white, and the blues in the water are deep and clear. The icebergs are also amazing because of their size and their forms. They can be huge or small, but each one has a unique shape. Moreover, you can walk on new snow that stretches for miles. In short, the beauty of Antarctica cannot be matched anywhere else in the world.

Second, the sounds in Antarctica are amazing. They range from total silence to a cacophony.[2] The silence comes when you are by yourself on top of a hill and you hear nothing but a slight breeze. The noise comes when you are standing next to a thousand penguins, especially when they are sitting on their nests or caring for their  babies. Penguins form families, and they recognize each other through their caws.[3] Each one sounds unique to a penguin, but to a human, it is just loud.

The most wondrous feeling you get in Antarctica is the sense that you are seeing something that is completely new. You have become the explorer of new land. The penguins and the seals are not afraid of you. You can stand there, and the penguins walk around you. The seals don't move as you walk around them. You realize that there is still a place on our hugely populated and industrialized Earth that is new. It's an amazing feeling.

---

[1]**eco-cruise** n. a cruise to an area where you can see the beauty of nature without harming it

[2]**cacophony** n. a loud mixture of sounds
[3]**caw** n. the sound of a bird

The Water Around Us

I VOCABULARY BUILDER

Use the nouns in the box below in the sentences. Work with a classmate.

cloud	ice	lake	ocean	rain	river	vapor

1. When water freezes, it becomes _____.

2. A _____ starts high in the mountains and flows down into the wide _____.

3. When the sun heats the ocean, some of the surface water rises as _____.

4. When the vapor rises from the ocean, it forms _____s in the sky.

5. When the clouds cannot hold the vapor any longer, the water falls on the Earth as _____.

6. Large bodies of fresh water on land are called _____s.

Now write the noun you think fits best in the spaces in the drawing below.

The Water Cycle

Concrete Support

One of the main challenges in essay writing is finding good ideas to support your thesis statement. Without sufficient support, an essay is not convincing. Professors who teach writing in the United States often say that their students (whether they are native speakers of English or not) especially need to work on the development of their arguments and to make sure that their support is strong and relevant.

In Chapter 2, you practiced writing paragraphs that had good coherence, cohesion, and unity. Practicing coherence and cohesion skills helps you write organized paragraphs. Practicing unity helps you make sure every sentence in your paragraph is relevant.

Essays are no different from paragraphs. When you write the body paragraphs of your essays, think about and write concrete support for your thesis statement that is well organized, relevant, and convincing. Convince your reader with specific facts, examples, and anecdotes.

Like the stand-alone paragraphs you have written before, the body paragraphs of an essay need to have good internal organization. In the following section you will practice writing topic sentences for the body paragraphs in an essay.

Topic Sentences in the Body Paragraphs of Essays

As you learned in Chapter 5, a good thesis statement consists of a topic and a controlling idea. The topic sentences of the body paragraphs in your essay support this controlling idea. For example, notice how these topic sentences support the thesis statement:

Thesis statement:	Pollution, waste, and climate change are threatening freshwater supplies.
Topic sentence 1:	Fresh water is being polluted by dirty water from several sources.
Topic sentence 2:	People are wasting fresh water.
Topic sentence 3:	Changes in global weather patterns have affected supplies of fresh water.

In this essay:

- The first body paragraph would explain how some businesses and factories are polluting lakes and rivers.

- The second body paragraph would explain some different ways people waste water.

- The third body paragraph would describe how global warming is causing some water supplies to disappear.

All of these support the thesis statement that pollution, waste, and climate change are threatening fresh water supplies.

■ **PRACTICE 1:** Writing Topic Sentences for Body Paragraphs

In pairs or small groups, discuss and decide on the missing body paragraph topic sentences. Write your choices on the lines provided.

1. *Essay title:* **Frozen Water: The Joys of Winter**

   Thesis statement: Growing up, my favorite time of year was winter because of the ice and snow.

   Topic sentence 1: We ice-skated for hours on the frozen lakes.

   Topic sentence 2: _____

   Topic sentence 3: My most beautiful memories are of snow-covered fields without a single track of an animal or a person.

2. *Essay title:* **The Water Cycle**

   Thesis statement: The stages of the cycle of water have not changed since the Earth formed.

   Topic sentence 1: _____

   Topic sentence 2: Next, the rainwater forms rivers, lakes, and oceans.

   Topic sentence 3: As the water surface heats up, it rises and turns into vapor.

   Topic sentence 4: When the vapor hits colder temperatures, it becomes clouds.

3. *Essay title:* **Bottled Water**

   Thesis statement: Buying and drinking bottled water is crazy.

   Topic sentence 1: _____

   Topic sentence 2: _____

   Topic sentence 3: Third, the millions of used plastic water bottles remain almost forever in our garbage dumps.

Bridges

Sometimes you may not need a topic sentence for each body paragraph. This can happen when the thesis statement for the essay has a predictor and clearly shows what the topic for each paragraph will be. Look at this thesis statement. Can you predict the number and content of the body paragraphs?

➤ There are three actions anyone can take to help decrease our garbage problem: Reduce the amount you throw away, reuse items that are still good, and recycle things that can be recycled.

This thesis statement indicates by its predictor that there will be three body paragraphs in this essay and that they will deal with reducing, reusing, and recycling. Those three body paragraphs will come in the order mentioned in the thesis statement. Because the predictor makes the topic of each body paragraph clear, the topic sentences are no longer necessary. Of course, you may still want to include them. It's your decision as the writer. It's important to remember, however, that each body paragraph must still be unified. This is especially true if there is no topic sentence.

If the first sentence of a body paragraph is not a topic sentence, it may function as a connection, or **bridge**, between one paragraph and another. In turn, if the first sentence is a bridge, then the second sentence could be a topic sentence.

In addition, concluding sentences in body paragraphs are not always required. The last sentence of a body paragraph may also function as a bridge to the following paragraph. In short, bridges can come at the beginning or end of a paragraph to make the cohesion of your essay better.

■ **PRACTICE 2:** Analyzing the First and Last Sentences in Body Paragraphs

Read the following essay. Underline the first and last sentence in each body paragraph. Then work with a classmate to answer the questions below.

1. What is the function of the first sentence in each body paragraph? Is it a topic sentence? Is it a bridge from the previous paragraph? If it is a bridge, is there a topic sentence after the bridge?

2. What is the purpose of the last sentence in each body paragraph? Is it a concluding sentence? Is it a bridge to the following paragraph?

Threats[1] to Our Ocean

Fish has been an important food source for people all over the world. It is high in protein, low in fat, and has many essential vitamins. However, these days, getting fish from the ocean may be damaging both the ocean and its future. Ocean fishing now is big business, so fishing companies want to get as much fish as possible from the ocean. However, their methods, such as overfishing, fish farming, and bottom trawling, are threats to our oceans.

Overfishing is a major problem. It happens when modern, technologically advanced ships hunt for fish. With the equipment on board, these ships can immediately find schools[2] of fish and get them all. In fact, these ships remove fish from the ocean faster that the ocean can replace them. Another problem with overfishing is that the nets catch more than fish. They also trap[3] whales, dolphins, and even birds, which are then destroyed.

Some people think that fish farming is the answer to overfishing in the ocean. However, fish farming is also damaging the ocean. For example, a typical salmon farm raises thousands of fish. To feed these fish, other, smaller fish are removed from the ocean in huge quantities. In fact, it requires five pounds of ocean fish to produce one pound of salmon. It's clear that fish farming is not the answer.

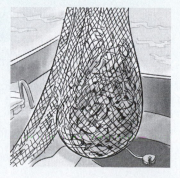

Bottom trawling is a term that describes catching fish at the bottom of the ocean. This happens when ships lower huge nets to the bottom of the ocean.

(continued)

The nets have wheels, which destroy everything they run over. The nets take everything, and a lot of what is brought up cannot be eaten. Moreover, the balance of diverse life that lives there is destroyed. Scientists say that there are still many, many kinds of undiscovered animals that live there. When they are brought to the surface, many are just thrown away.

In conclusion, our oceans provide us with many benefits, one of which is fish. We need to be careful, however, that our desire for fish doesn't destroy the ocean. Big fishing companies must find alternatives to their practices of overfishing, fish farming, and bottom trawling. If not, we may some day run out of the fish we desire.

> **What about you?**
>
> What are some other threats to the ocean? Share your ideas with a classmate.

Convincing Your Reader

Your essay needs to be logically developed so that your readers find it convincing. Convince your readers by giving them facts, examples, and anecdotes.

■ PRACTICE 3: Analyzing the Concrete Support Used in an Essay

Below is an essay about the ownership of water. There are two parts to this exercise.

- For the first part, you need three different colors of highlighters or pens. (You can also underline or circle the parts.) Read the essay and use one color to indicate something that is a statement of fact, another color to show something that is an example, and your third color to highlight an anecdote in each of the three body paragraphs. Discuss your answers with your classmates.

- Second, continue your discussion by answering these questions:
  1. Which of the arguments in the essay do you find most convincing?
  2. Why is it convincing?

Who Owns the Water?

I grew up and still live on a farm in San Fernando Valley, California. We grow vegetables, and the acres of vegetables need constant water. That is our problem: While the soil in San Fernando Valley is very good for growing vegetables, we get very little natural rainfall. As a result, our farming depends on irrigation[1].  Water for irrigation needs to come from far away, and many other people also think they need that water. Who has the right to water? Clearly, those who provide food (like my family) have a stronger right to the water than those who live nearest to it or those who can afford to pay the most for it.

The rivers that farmers use for irrigation begin in the mountains to the east, and the people who live there want to dam[2] the river. They argue that they have a right to create a dam and stop the river to create a recreational park. The park will bring tourists and much-needed money. However, the farmers in the San Fernando Valley use the water to grow fruits and vegetables to feed the state's population. By irrigating fields, farmers can harvest[3] two times a year. Without irrigation, they can only harvest once. People need recreation, but people need food more.

Other people argue that water belongs to anyone who can pay for it. For example, the people in the desert town of Santa Andrea have enormous houses with large green lawns. To keep their lawns green, they water their grass all night, every night. One millionaire even has a series of swimming pools from which he empties all the water every evening and, because of an automatic system to fill them with fresh water overnight, they are full again every morning! However, where would the rich people of Santa Andrea get their food if we didn't grow their vegetables for them? They can't eat their lawns.

In conclusion, the question of ownership of water is a complex one, but everyone—the farmers, the dam builders, and the wealthy—can agree that fresh water is a precious resource on Earth. In my opinion, that fresh water must go first to the farmers. Unlike the other groups, farmers are serving all of the people in the state.

[1]**irrigation** *n.* bringing water to the plants in a field

[2]**dam** *v.* to build a structure across a river to stop the water from flowing

[3]**harvest** *v.* to gather fruits, vegetables, and grains from plants

■ **PRACTICE 4: Writing a Body Paragraph**

The essay below has one body paragraph missing. Write the missing paragraph by yourself. Then share your new paragraph with one or two classmates. How are your paragraphs similar? How are they different?

Water Is Life

Excited scientists have recently discovered water on Mars. Their excitement is understandable. The existence of water indicates life. Indeed, water is life. However, here on Earth, water is so plentiful for most of us that we take it for granted. Water in its three states—vapor, liquid, and solid—allows us not only to live, but to enjoy living.

(continued)

First of all, hot water vapor, or steam, is a very good conductor of heat. Steam is created by boiling water, and then it used for many purposes. For example, we can use steam to cook vegetables, and steaming vegetables is the best way to maintain their vitamins. We also use steam to clean fabrics, such as clothes and carpets. Heating buildings with steam is also quite common. We even use steam to power engines.

_____

_____

_____

_____.

Finally, water in its solid form of ice is invaluable in food preparation and in recreation. Ice keeps our drinks cool, but more importantly, it helps preserve[1] food for use at a later time. In addition, we use ice in many sports. Children in cold climates grow up skating on a frozen pond or lake. Ice in the form of snow provides people with hours of fun while skiing or snow boarding.

In short, it is impossible to live without water, so it is important to occasionally acknowledge its importance to us. With water as a vapor, a liquid, and a solid, our lives are safer and more enjoyable.

[1]**preserve** *v.* to keep someone or something from being harmed, destroyed, or changed too much

III STRUCTURE AND MECHANICS

Avoiding Comma Splices

In the last chapter, you learned to avoid run-on sentences. A similar type of error is called a **comma splice**. Like a run-on sentence, a comma splice is formed when two independent clauses are not separated correctly. A comma splice results when there is only a comma between the two independent clauses. Look at this example of a comma splice:

➤ Our oceans are in danger, there is too much overfishing.

As with run-on sentences, there are five ways to correct comma splices:

1. Make two separate sentences

   ➤ Our oceans are in danger. There is too much overfishing.

2. Add a coordinating conjunction (see Chapter 1)

   ➤ Our oceans are in danger, **for** there is too much overfishing.

   ➤ There is too much overfishing, **so** our oceans are in danger.

3. Add a subordinating conjunction (see Chapter 3)

➤ Our oceans are in danger **because** there is too much overfishing.

➤ **Because** there is too much overfishing, our oceans are in danger.

4. Add a transition (see Chapter 4)

➤ There is too much overfishing. **Therefore,** our oceans are in danger.

➤ There is too much overfishing; **therefore,** our oceans are in danger.

5. Make one independent clause into a prepositional phrase (see Chapter 5)

➤ **Because of** too much overfishing, our oceans are in danger.

➤ Our oceans are in danger **because of** too much overfishing.

■ **PRACTICE 5:** **Correcting Comma Splices**

This paragraph has five comma splices. Find them and underline them. Then rewrite the paragraph with corrections on another piece of paper. Try to correct the comma splices by using each of the five ways explained above.

The Power of Water

When I was a boy, my father and I wanted to get rid of some huge rocks near our house in the countryside, my mother wanted to plant a vegetable garden. The rocks were enormous, we couldn't move them. Unfortunately, we didn't have the equipment to move such heavy objects. We decided to use an ancient method. We waited until winter, then we built a fire around some of the largest rocks. That made them crack a little bit. That wasn't enough, in the evening, we poured water into those cracks and left. The water froze overnight since water expands when it turns to ice, by the next morning, the large rocks had cracked into smaller pieces. We could easily carry away the smaller pieces. In short, water beats rock every time!

IV WRITING TO COMMUNICATE

Your Turn

In this assignment, you are going to develop your first complete essay. Review the steps outlined in Appendix 1 on page 173.

Step 1: Analyzing the Assignment

Here's what your professor said:

Write a four- or five-paragraph essay on ways water can be used for fun and enjoyment. You may work with other students if you wish; however, you should do your own writing. Your essay is due _____. I will accept a hard copy in class or a copy attached to an e-mail.

Be sure that you understand the assignment before you move on.

Step 2: Brainstorming

In small groups or pairs, discuss the possible ways you could respond to the assignment. Practice brainstorming in any way that you like. While you may get ideas from your classmates, you should write your own notes.

Step 3: Organizing Your Ideas

Narrow your topic, eliminating irrelevant ideas and adding relevant ones. Write your thesis statement and make an outline. Follow this one if you like.

Thesis statement

➤ _____

_____

Topic of body paragraph 1

➤ _____

Topic of body paragraph 2

➤ _____

Topic of body paragraph 3

➤ _____

Step 4: Writing the First Draft

Follow your outline to write the first draft. It may be easier if you write the body paragraphs first. Then write the introductory and concluding paragraph.

Step 5: Rewriting the First Draft

Put your essay away for at least 30 minutes and then reread it. If you have a classmate to work with, read each other's essays and comment on them for each other. If you don't have anyone else to work with, read your own essay as if someone else had written it. Be critical! Think of these questions for revision first:

- Do you need a few more examples?

- Should you shorten or lengthen an anecdote?

- Does everything in your body paragraphs support your thesis statement and help the reader understand your position?

Next, edit your essay by looking critically at your language, spelling, and punctuation. Look at the words you have chosen and see if you can find synonyms for words you have used too many times. If you type your essay, use the spell checker function, but be careful: the spell checker does not know the difference between *their, they're,* and *there.* Check your nouns: Have you used the proper definite and indefinite articles? Read your verbs: Are they in the correct tense?

Step 6: Writing the Final Paper (or Next Draft)

Write your final draft. Use good paragraph format, including your name and the date in the upper right-hand corner. Your teacher might also ask you to include the name of the course and the name of the class. That's it—congratulations! You have completed your first academic essay.

Peer Help Worksheet

Trade essays and textbooks with a classmate. Read your classmate's essay while your classmate reads yours. Check off (✔) the items in your partner's book as you evaluate them. Then return the essays and books. If any of the items in your book are not checked off, and you agree with your partner, correct your essay before turning it in. Use a pencil if you write on your classmate's essay or book.

CONTENT

1 What did you find most interesting about this essay?

2 What type of support is used in this essay? (Check all that apply.)

   a. facts . . . . ❑

   b. examples . . . . ❑

   c. anecdotes . . . . ❑

ORGANIZATION

1 Does the essay have a thesis statement with these elements?

   a. Topic (If so, circle it.) . . . . ❑

   b. Controlling idea (If so, underline it.) . . . . ❑

   c. Predictor (If so, put a box around it.) . . . . ❑

2 How many body paragraphs does this essay have? _____

   a. Does each have a topic sentence? If so, underline it. . . . . ❑

      If *no*, is it clear from the thesis statement what the topic of this paragraph is? . . . . ❑

   b. What is the function of the last sentence in each body paragraph?

      • a true concluding sentence. . . . . ❑

      • a bridge to the next paragraph . . . . ❑

MECHANICS

1 Is this essay written with correct paragraph format? . . . . ❑

2 Do you think there are any comma splices that need to be corrected? . . . . ❑

   If so, point them out to your classmate.

Writing to Communicate . . . More

For more writing practice, write an essay about one of these topics. For further help with the writing process, see Appendix 1 on page 173.

1. Describe one or more sports played in water or on snow or ice.

2. Many parts of the Earth have land for agriculture, but the lack of water makes it very difficult to grow food. Write an essay about methods of irrigation that you are familiar with. You may include both historical and modern methods.

3. Would you prefer to live by a lake, a river, or an ocean? Write an essay that states and explains your preference.

PART II — BRINGING IT ALL TOGETHER

I | REVIEWING TERMS

Answer these questions about the essay on page 110.

1. What type of introductory paragraph does this essay have? (Check one.)

   ❏ general to specific   ❏ anecdote   ❏ historical

2. What parts does the thesis statement have? (Check all that apply.)

   ❏ topic (Circle it.)

   ❏ controlling idea (Underline it.)

   ❏ predictor (Put a box around it.)

3. What type of support is used to convince the reader? (Check all that apply.) Give an example of each type that you find.

   ❏ facts   _____

   ❏ examples   _____

   ❏ anecdotes   _____

4. What is the function of the first sentence in each body paragraph? (Check one for each paragraph.)

   Body paragraph 1: ❏ topic sentence   ❏ bridge   ❏ neither

   Body paragraph 2: ❏ topic sentence   ❏ bridge   ❏ neither

   Body paragraph 3: ❏ topic sentence   ❏ bridge   ❏ neither

5. What is the function of the last sentence in each body paragraph? (Check one for each paragraph.)

   Body paragraph 1: ❏ concluding sentence   ❏ bridge   ❏ neither

   Body paragraph 2: ❏ concluding sentence   ❏ bridge   ❏ neither

   Body paragraph 3: ❏ concluding sentence   ❏ bridge   ❏ neither

6. What components does the concluding paragraph have? (Check all that apply.)

   ❏ restatement of the thesis statement

   ❏ summary of the body of the essay

   ❏ final comment

Greenpeace: Defender of the Environment

The Greenpeace Foundation is an organization of ordinary people and scientists from around the world who find solutions to global environmental problems. The organization was started in the early 1970s to defend human, animal, and plant life. Today, Greenpeace continues to protect the environment by exposing[1] illegal fishing, saving old forests, and reducing the pollution of our air and water.

There are countless coastal communities around the world. The people living in these communities survive by fishing off their shores. However, the serious problem of illegal fishing has decreased the amount of fish that is available in these places. This type of fishing is called pirate fishing because ships that do this steal fish in huge quantities and leave the water nearly empty of fish. To combat[2] this practice, Greenpeace is making a list of these ships so that countries will know whether or not the fish they are buying is legal. Other Greenpeace activities are much more personal, however.

Ancient forests are forest areas that are mostly undisturbed by people. One example of an ancient forest is the Great Bear Rain Forest, which covers western Canada. This forest was damaged by clear-cutting, which means that every single tree in a large area is cut down at the same time. The clear-cutting seriously harmed the population of grizzly bears and salmon. Greenpeace members put themselves between the trees and the tree cutters. They experienced a victory on August 26, 1999, when the U.S. company Home Depot, a major buyer of wood from the Great Bear Rain Forest, announced that it would stop selling wood products from rain forests. Although this was only a small step in the process of protecting the forests we have left, it was still a significant event.

However, the major threat to plants, animals, and people is neither pirate fishing nor clear-cutting but the extremely toxic[3] chemicals released into the air and water. Greenpeace has helped local people protest against companies that produce such pollution. One small victory happened in Louisiana in the late 1990s. For three years, a plastics company had tried to establish PVC[4] factories next to schools and homes in the small town of Convent, Louisiana. PVC is a common type of plastic used in everything from children's toys to kitchen containers. PVC itself is safe, but its manufacturing produces dioxin, an extremely toxic chemical. With the help of Greenpeace, the citizens of Convent won their battle in September of 1998, when the plastics company withdrew its plans to build the factories.

In conclusion, each victory[5] gives us hope, but they are small when contrasted with the problems we face. Even so, Greenpeace activists fight on, and their efforts in preventing pirate fishing, protecting ancient forests, and limiting the use of dangerous chemicals are showing some positive effects. Because of Greenpeace, the world will be a little safer for our children and our children's children.

[1]**expose** *v.* to show something that is usually covered or hidden
[2]**combat** *v.* to try to stop something bad from happening or getting worse
[3]**toxic** *adj.* poisonous
[4]**PVC** *n.* an abbreviation for polyvinyl chloride
[5]**victory** *n.* the success you achieve by winning a battle, game, or election

II ERROR ANALYSIS

Analyze and mark the sentences below.

- Write *C* in the blank if the sentence is correct.
- Write *F* if the sentence is a fragment.
- Write *RO* if the sentence is a run-on sentence.
- Write *CS* if the sentence has a comma splice.

Then correct the sentences that have mistakes. Compare your corrections with a classmate.

——— 1. Some animals don't have sufficient shelter their predators can easily kill them.

——— 2. My eyesight may be fuzzy, my hearing is keen.

——— 3. After George inherited a farm in Oklahoma.

——— 4. Julia is proud of the fact that she's been to all seven continents.

——— 5. Oceans, lakes, and ponds are bodies of water, a river is an example of water in motion.

——— 6. When I opened the door and smelled the air, I knew my mom was cooking my favorite meal.

——— 7. Traveling in the desert last summer in our old truck.

——— 8. Bruce is a storm chaser he will go anywhere at anytime to try to get a picture of a tornado.

——— 9. The Arctic tundra is one of the coldest places on the Earth, yet it is also one of the most beautiful in my opinion.

——— 10. There are many endangered species in the world, the cockroach is not one of them.

PART III

RHETORICAL PATTERNS

PROCESS

A Healthy Mind in a Healthy Body

I VOCABULARY BUILDER

Look at the list of words in the chart. Discuss their meaning with a classmate and your teacher. Use a dictionary if necessary. Then look at the pictures on page 115. Which of the words in the chart do you associate with each picture? Write them on the lines. Words can be used more than once. Then share your ideas with a classmate.

What about you?

What type of exercise do you do on a regular basis? Share your answer with a classmate.

WORDS ABOUT EXERCISE

Nouns	Adjectives	Verbs
couple	aerobic	climb
endurance	coordinated	dance
heart rate	individual	jog
pace	rhythmic	stretch
stamina	steady	swing

_____   _____   _____   _____
_____   _____   _____   _____
_____   _____   _____   _____
_____   _____   _____   _____
_____   _____   _____   _____

II WRITING FOCUS

Process

In this chapter, you will practice writing essays that describe a **process**. A process is a series of events or steps that are orderly and predictable. You can describe a process in the past, such as how something happened; a process in the present, such as how something works; or a process in the future, such as how to do something. A process essay describes the steps or stages in the change of something into something else. To write this type of essay well, it is important to make sure that all the steps are covered and that they are presented in chronological order.

Graphic Organizers

The number of paragraphs in a process essay depends on how you organize your information. Some essays are very simple and have only three paragraphs: an introduction, a long body paragraph, and a conclusion. Other essays may have two, three, or even more body paragraphs.

Graphic Organizer 1

Introductory paragraph

Thesis statement

Long body paragraph

All the steps in the correct chronological order

First steps

↓

Last steps

Concluding paragraph

Essay conclusion

Graphic Organizer 2

Introductory paragraph

Thesis statement

Body paragraph 1

Components, tools, and equipment

Body paragraph 2

Description of the process step-by-step

First step

↓

Next step

↓

(Next step)

etc.

Concluding paragraph

Essay conclusion

Graphic Organizer 3

Introductory paragraph

Thesis statement

Body paragraph 1

Components, tools, and equipment

OR

The first part of the process

Body paragraph 2

The first (or next) step of the process

Body paragraph 3

The next steps of the process

(More body paragraphs as needed)

The end of the process

Concluding paragraph

Essay conclusion

Model Essay 1

A Change of Heart

His Holiness the Dalai Lama has said that all human beings seek happiness and freedom from suffering. However, what brings happiness and joy? From my experience, what gives you the most pleasure varies a lot with the kind of person you are, but it also depends on your stage of life. Our concept of happiness goes through five stages as we mature.

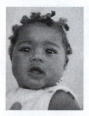

In the first stage of life, our happiness depends mostly on family ties. A child needs security and attachment to one or more adults to be happy. Babies gaze[1] adoringly into the eyes of their mothers because that's what makes them happy. When children smile at their parents and their parents smile back, they feel safe and loved. Parents are their entire world. However, we don't remain babies; we grow into the next stage of life.

(continued)

As children become teenagers, they often try to distance themselves from the family that previously was their entire universe. In Western cultures, parents almost expect their teenager to be rebellious.[2] Nevertheless, in all cultures teenagers seek other people their own age outside their families, and they find their happiness primarily in socializing with their friends.

In the next stage, early adulthood, our concept of happiness changes again. At this stage, most people seek attachment to one special person. This expectation and desire to find happiness in a romantic attachment is so strong in some cultures that people feel unhappy if they don't find it. In other cultures, mutual respect between marriage partners is more highly valued than romantic love, but the attachment between the two people is just as strong.

As they enter a later stage of adulthood, many people begin to expand their views. They move from only seeking happiness from a two-person relationship to seeking fulfillment from achievements and social relations. Their circle grows wider, including long-term friends as well as an extended family, and many people focus intensely on achieving career goals. Because most people are also financially better off at this stage, many begin to travel, and they find a lot of satisfaction in meeting and forming relationships with people from other cultures.

Finally, in the last stage of life, we mature into old age, and the idea of what brings us happiness often changes again. At this stage, many people begin to realize that possessions and money didn't really bring lasting happiness. They seek happiness in self-actualization[3] through helping others, through artistic efforts, or from spirituality.

In conclusion, the baby looks for happiness in the intimate contact with loving parents, but teenagers seek to break the bonds which held them so tight. While young adults look for happiness through a perfect mate, older adults often seek enjoyment in recognition of their achievements or in friends, and mature adults tend to look for personal or spiritual satisfaction. As we live through the stages of life, we change, and change, although never easy, is the spice of life.

[1] **gaze** *v.* to look intently at something   [2] **rebellious** *adj.* disobedient   [3] **self-actualization** *n.* successful personal development

■ **PRACTICE 1: Analyzing Model Essay 1**

With a classmate, discuss the answers to these questions about Model Essay 1.

1. Does the thesis statement have these things? (Check all that apply.)
   ❑ clear topic
   ❑ controlling idea
   ❑ predictor

2. How many steps are in the process?

3. Which organizational pattern is used in the essay?

Model Essay 2

Culture Shock

I moved to another country when I was eighteen, and I have now lived there for ten years. By now, it is very comfortable for me to live in my new country. Although I was happy at first, after a while I began to feel miserable. Luckily for me, a friend of mine showed me how the process of adjusting to a new culture goes through distinct stages. Her explanations made me feel more secure because then I could predict how I would feel about my new home. According to my friend's explanation, there are four stages of cultural adjustment.

Initially, you feel happy in the new environment. It's new and it's exciting. You think that everything here is better than where you were before. My friend called this the "honeymoon" stage. The second stage comes very quickly, and it's almost unavoidable. Your initial love affair with your new country quickly turns to hate. Suddenly, you start to see everything that seems wrong with this country. It could be the traffic, the way people smile or don't smile, the customs about paying attention to time, or even the food. My friend told me that this unhappy feeling was quite natural and that I ought to notice it, but that I shouldn't pay too much attention to it. If I could just hold on and survive this culture shock period, she said I would arrive at the next stage: acceptance. This is the stage in which you realize that your new country is truly different from the one in which you grew up, but that there are no rights and wrongs in culture. It just is. Once you accept that, you can keep working toward your goals. However, she also said that there was a fourth stage, which she called the "at home" stage. At this stage, you feel at home in the new country, and you feel completely comfortable with your daily life. You know how to do small things like buy a newspaper, fill your car with gas, or book an airplane flight over the telephone.

(continued)

To sum up, the four stages of cultural adjustment made a lot of sense to me, and I have passed through every one. However, what my friend didn't tell me is that when you return to your native country, you are very likely to go through the stages all over again! I have heard this called "re-entry shock." Knowing this helps me a lot as I travel back and forth between my native country and my adopted country.

■ **PRACTICE 2: Analyzing Model Essay 2**

With a classmate, discuss the answers to these questions about Model Essay 2.

1. Does the thesis statement have these things? (Check all that apply.)
   - ❑ clear topic
   - ❑ controlling idea
   - ❑ predictor

2. How many steps are in the process?

3. Which organizational pattern is used in the essay?

Model Essay 3

How to Gain Fifty Pounds

When we are born, we all weigh between six and ten pounds. Nevertheless, as we grow, some of us increase to 300 pounds and some of us only to 100 pounds. Why does this happen? Part of it has to do with genetics and whether our genes tell us to grow tall and big or short and slim. On the other hand, a large part of the difference also has to do with our habits. It's not difficult to gain weight if you follow these steps.

You only need two ingredients to gain weight: less activity and more food. The body is a rather simple machine. It takes in fuel in the form of food, and it burns fuel through exercise. If the body takes in more fuel from the calories in food than it burns off in living and exercising, it will store the extra calories as body fat.

The first step in the process of gaining weight is to decrease your daily level of activities. For example, if you usually walk to work or school, you can drive instead. Make sure you park very close to your workplace so you don't have to move much, and take the elevator instead of the stairs. If you usually enjoy a game of tennis or like to jog, stop! Remember that aerobic exercise is your enemy. Every way you can find to decrease the amount of calories you burn will help you add more pounds. Secondly, you need to consume as many calories as you can. If you usually eat a lot of vegetables or fruits, that makes it hard. In order to gain weight, you need the kind of food that has a large amount of calories per gram. For that reason, if you eat a doughnut or three for breakfast instead of a bowl of cereal with milk, you'll be sure to gain weight. Similarly, if you substitute a double cheeseburger for your normal lunchtime apple and yogurt, you'll gain even more. Finally, make sure to drink a lot of sugary soft drinks with your meal.

As you can see, gaining weight is easy. You may not like all that fat and sugar in the beginning, but if you work at it, you'll get quite used to it. By following these steps, I promise you can gain fifty pounds in a year.

■ PRACTICE 3: Analyzing Model Essay 3

With a classmate, discuss the answers to these questions about Model Essay 3.

1. Does the thesis statement have these things? (Check all that apply.)
   - ❏ clear topic
   - ❏ controlling idea
   - ❏ predictor
2. How many steps are in the process?
3. Which organizational pattern is used in the essay?
4. Why do you think the writer chose to write about this serious topic (weight gain) in a humorous way?

■ PRACTICE 4: Ordering the Steps in a Process

Daniel feels that his life is too busy. He wants to calm down. He wants to practice meditation. What are his first steps in learning how to meditate?

Write the numbers 1 through 7 in the exercise below. Then compare the order for the steps you chose with a classmate. If your answers are different, discuss the reasons for your choices.

	My Choices	**My Classmate's**
Pay attention to your breath.	_____	_____
Open your eyes.	_____	_____
If your mind wanders, focus again on your breath.	_____	_____
Find a quiet place to sit.	_____	_____
Start to breathe slowly.	_____	_____
Close your eyes.	_____	_____
Notice how you've become calmer.	_____	_____

Chronological Connectors

As you know, connectors join sentences and improve the relationship of ideas in a text. There are several different types of connectors: transitions, conjunctions, and prepositions. This chart reviews the different type of connectors and provides a list of some common ones used in essays that describe a process.

Chronological Connectors			
Purpose		**Common Linking Words**	**Sample Sentences**
Transitions	*connect two independent clauses*	first second next then after that at this point later on finally	Sue played basketball. **After that,** she played tennis.
Conjunctions — Subordinating	*introduce adverb clauses*	after before since when while	**After** Sue played basketball, she played tennis. Sue played tennis **after** she played basketball.
Conjunctions — Coordinating	*connect two independent clauses*	and	Sue played basketball, **and** she played tennis.
Prepositions	*precede nouns or noun phrases*	after before in addition to prior to since	**After** playing basketball, Sue played tennis. Sue played tennis **after** playing basketball.

■ **PRACTICE 5: Adding Connectors**

Read the ten steps below describing the process of making scrambled eggs. Then write a complete paragraph using the sentences and the connectors in parentheses.

Note that the steps are in the imperative. When a subordinating conjunction is used, you will need to change the imperative verb. Use *you* as the subject and a present tense verb in the adverb clause. For example:

➤ Pour milk into the glass. Add chocolate syrup. *(before)*

Pour milk into the glass before you add chocolate syrup.

1. Break three eggs in a bowl.
2. Mix them using a wire whisk.
3. Add one tablespoon of water for each egg.
4. Add a pinch of salt.
5. Heat a frying pan.
6. Melt one tablespoon of butter in the pan.
7. Pour in the egg mixture.
8. Stir the eggs by scraping the pan with a spatula.
9. Stop scraping when the eggs are golden yellow.
10. Don't overcook the eggs. Cooking eggs too long makes them rubbery.

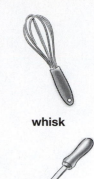

whisk

spatula

Sentence 1 *(first)*

_____

Sentence 2 *(next)*

_____

Sentences 3 and 4 *(after)* (*Note:* Change the imperative verb.)

_____

Sentence 5 *(at this point)*

_____

Sentences 6 and 7 *(after)* (*Note:* Change the imperative verb.)

_____

Sentences 8 and 9 *(until)*

_____

Sentence 10 *(finally)*

_____

Reviewing Comma Use

You have learned how to use commas correctly with coordinating conjunctions (page 13), in lists (page 27), with adverbial clauses (page 41), with transitions (page 58), and with prepositional phrases (page 72). Practice 6 reviews of all these uses of a comma.

■ *PRACTICE 6:* **Using Commas in a Process Paragraph**

Insert commas in the correct places in this paragraph. The paragraph needs 12 commas.

Training for My First Marathon

My year of training for my first marathon consisted of three stages. First of all I needed to improve my strength so I started going to a gym every day. I did anaerobic exercises with free weights took a weightlifting class and even climbed the gym's rock wall. At this point I started working on my flexibility. I added yoga to my exercise routine. After a few months I really noticed a difference. Without any difficulty I could stretch far enough to touch the floor. My third stage was an emphasis on stamina. After I started jogging every morning my resting heart rate was slowing down and I was breathing better. The aerobic nature of jogging really helped me. At the end of my year in training I finally felt brave enough to register for the marathon. I never thought it would be possible but I actually competed in a marathon last year and it was great!

IV WRITING TO COMMUNICATE

Your Turn

Your process essay assignment for this chapter is *How to stay physically healthy.* Start by brainstorming with your classmates the many aspects of physical health. For example, ask yourselves questions like these:

- Does the food we eat matter?

- Does it matter when we eat it?

- What kinds of exercises should we do?

- How can we avoid illness?

Second, select the aspects of physical health you want to write about. Now organize your ideas in an outline and start planning your thesis statement. Some people write the thesis statement and the body paragraphs first and the introduction and conclusion afterward. Then read through your essay and revise it as necessary. At this point, exchange your essay with a classmate and use the Peer Help Worksheet to give each other feedback. Finally, with your classmate's comments and your own ideas, edit your essay and write the final draft, paying special attention to punctuation and capitalization.

Peer Help Worksheet

Trade essays and textbooks with a classmate. Read your classmate's essay while your classmate reads yours. Check off (✓) the items in your partner's book as you evaluate them. Then return the essays and books. If any of the items in your book are not checked off, and you agree with your partner, correct your essay before turning it in. Use a pencil if you write on your classmate's essay or book.

CONTENT

What did you like most about this essay?

ORGANIZATION

1 What does the thesis statement contain? (Check all that apply.)

   a. topic . . . . ❑

   b. controlling idea . . . . ❑

   c. predictor . . . . ❑

2 What does the introduction contain? (Check one.)

   a. anecdote . . . . ❑

   b. historical information . . . . ❑

   c. general to specific organization . . . . ❑

3 How many steps are listed in the process? _____

   Are they in the correct order? . . . . ❑

4 What does the concluding paragraph do? (Check all that apply.)

   a. restates the thesis . . . . ❑

   b. summarizes the steps . . . . ❑

   c. gives a final comment . . . . ❑

MECHANICS

1 How many of the following connectors are there in this essay?

   (Write the number in the blank.)

   a. coordinating conjunctions   _____

   b. subordinating conjunctions   _____

   c. transitions   _____

2 Do you think commas are used correctly with each of these? . . . ❑

   If not, discuss any possible mistakes with the writer.

Writing to Communicate . . . More

Process writing can be long and complicated, or it can be short and simple. It can be a whole book (e.g., Dale Carnegie's *How to Win Friends and Influence People*), a medium-length article in a magazine ("How to Lose 10 Pounds in 10 Days" or "How to Succeed in Business"), or just a list of steps to program your DVD player or set up an e-mail account. Following are some other topics that lend themselves to a process organizational pattern. Choose one and write an essay about it.

Sports and Games

All over the world, people play games in their free time. These games range from simple children's games, such as jumping rope, to complex adult games such as chess and tennis. Think of a simple sport or game and write an essay describing how to play it. Consider the following:

- What equipment do you need?

- What are the main rules of the game?

- How do you win the game?

Preparing For and Surviving Disasters

Natural disasters can happen anytime and anywhere. How can you be well prepared for such a disaster? What could you do before, during, and after it to increase your chances of survival? Choose from these natural disasters: earthquakes, mudslides, avalanches, hailstorms, tornadoes, hurricanes, floods, and snowstorms. Write an essay explaining how you can prepare for and survive this disaster. Consider the following:

- What supplies would you need to survive until help comes? (food, water, heat source, clothes, medical supplies, etc.)

- How can you make your home safe from a disaster?

- What kind of plan should you make to contact family or friends?

- What should you do and not do during the disaster?

- What are the first things to do to recover from the disaster?

Tongue-in-Cheek

Write a funny essay in which you describe how to do the opposite of what people usually want to do. Consider the following:

- How to fail a test

- How to be a boring person

- How to break up with your boyfriend or girlfriend

- How to make a lot of enemies

CHAPTER 10

CLASSIFICATION

Diversity Among People

I VOCABULARY BUILDER

We all have many sides to our personality. In addition, we react differently in different situations. Even so, some of our basic personality characteristics tend to stay fairly constant.

A. *Below are eight pairs of adjectives describing personality characteristics. Describe yourself using the words in each pair. Discuss your answers with a classmate.*

assertive/passive	daring/timid
ambitious/easygoing	organized/disorganized
cautious/reckless	outgoing/shy
creative/detail-oriented	stubborn/flexible

I am more _____ than I am _____.

I am more _____ than I am _____.

I am more _____ than I am _____.

I am more _____ than I am _____.

I am more _____ than I am _____.

I am more _____ than I am _____.

I am more _____ than I am _____.

I am more _____ than I am _____.

B. *Circle the adjective that best describes the personality of each person.*

1. Zuleia almost always says no to party invitations because she feels uncomfortable about meeting new people.

   a. disorganized   **b.** shy   **c.** passive

2. Maria Belen always agrees to do everything her husband wants to do—even when she doesn't want to do it.

   a. daring   **b.** stubborn   **c.** passive

3. When the Robinson family traveled to Asia last year, they spent six months planning the trip before they left.

   a. organized   **b.** assertive   **c.** easygoing

4. Adam read a lot of extra books and studied on the weekends because he wanted to get an A in the class.

   a. timid   **b.** ambitious   **c.** cautious

5. Paulo loves looking at a blank piece of paper and imagining what he could write on it, but he hates editing his writing.

   a. flexible   **b.** reckless   **c.** creative

II WRITING FOCUS

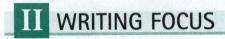

Classification

When you **classify**, you divide objects, people, or ideas into groups or categories. It is something we do constantly. You might organize movies into those you like and those you don't like; you might divide people you know into those who are outgoing and those who are quiet; you might classify music into classical, rock and roll, country, rap, and so on.

You always classify according to a **principle** even though you may not be aware of it. For example, consider the topic of *boats*. If you want to write an essay classifying boats, you will state the subject you are describing (*boats*), the classification principle (for example, *how they move*), and the categories (in this case, *sailboats, powerboats, rowboats*).

■ PRACTICE 1: Classifying People

Discuss with your classmates different ways you could classify people by filling in this chart. There are no correct answers; the answers will depend on the choices you make. One example has been done for you.

Subject	Classification Principle	Number of Categories	Category Names
People	*gender*	*2*	*male, female*
People	age		baby, child, adolescent, adult, senior citizen
People	education		
People			extrovert, introvert
People	body types	3	
People	hair color		
People	face shape		
People	occupation		
People			
People			

■ **PRACTICE 2: Determining the Classification Principle**

The classification principle is understood, but not stated, in these five thesis statements. Select a, b, or c as the understood classification principle. Then compare your answers with a classmate.

1. There are two types of high schools in the United States: public and private.
   a. quality of instruction
   b. qualification of the teachers
   c. payment for the school

2. Deep-sea fishing, shore fishing, and river fishing are the kinds of fishing most people enjoy.
   a. the size of the fish you catch
   b. where you do the fishing
   c. how much you like the activity

3. In the gym where I work out, there are front-row people, middle-of-the-room people, and back-row people.
   a. where they usually place themselves
   b. whether they are outgoing or shy
   c. their height

4. Mexican, Thai, and Italian are the three types of restaurants in my town.
   a. the nationality of the owner
   b. the type of food that is served
   c. the neighborhood the restaurant is in

■ **PRACTICE 3: Writing Classification Thesis Statements**

Look at the categories and principle for classifying each of the following three groups. Then write a thesis statement for each group.

For example:

| Subject: | Writers |
| Principle: | What they write |

| Categories: | *novelists* | *reporters* |
| | *poets* | *essayists* |

Thesis statement: *Novelists, reporters, poets, and essayists are four important but different kinds of writers.*

1. Subject: Athletes
   Principle: The kind of sports they play
   Categories: <u>*individual*</u> <u>*team*</u>
   Thesis statement: _____
   _____

2. Subject: Actors

     Principle: Where they act

     Categories: _____*movies*_____   _____*stage*_____

                          _____*TV*_____   _____

     Thesis statement: _____

     _____

3. Subject: Teachers

     Principle: Personality

     Categories: _____*strict*_____   _____*moderate*_____

                          _____*easygoing*_____   _____

     Thesis statement: _____

     _____

Paragraph Support in the Classification Essay

How do you turn a simple classification into a full-length essay? The best way is to choose detailed examples and descriptions to convince your reader that your categories are reasonable.

For example, imagine that you have divided the group "my friends" into three categories: *worrywarts* (people who worry all the time about everything), *bookworms* (people who study all the time), and *fatalists* (people who feel that life is outside their control). Your thesis statement is that all of your friends fall into one of these three groups.

To get started, define the categories. Next, show your reader exactly what makes the people in one group different from those in the other two. To do this, you may ask yourself some questions:

- How does this type of person act?
- How does this person feel and behave in certain situations in which the others would feel and behave very differently?
- How do I feel when I am with a person like this?

The answers to those kinds of questions will lead you to the illustrations you can use to support your thesis statement.

■ **PRACTICE 4:** Brainstorming Ideas for Paragraph Development

With your classmates, discuss what these three types of people do in the following situations. Write notes next to each category.

1. It's 8:00 A.M., and the writing class starts at 8:30 A.M. The bus should have left at 7:45 A.M., but it's late, and your friend won't get to class on time. What would this person do?

     a worrywart: _____

     a bookworm: *He would think that this is a great opportunity to reread the textbook*

                        lesson for that day.

     a fatalist: _____

(continued)

2. Your friend was in a car accident. He wasn't hurt badly, but the insurance company says it was his fault, and it won't insure your friend again next year. What would this person do?

a worrywart: _____

a bookworm: _____

a fatalist: _____

3. The TOEFL® test is two weeks from now. Your friend must get a high score to be admitted to her favorite college. What would this person do?

a worrywart: _____

a bookworm: _____

a fatalist: _____

Graphic Organizer

Organizing a classification essay is not difficult because each of the categories you've established becomes a body paragraph. The number of categories determines the number of body paragraphs.

Introduction

Thesis statement

Body paragraph 1

Description and illustration of category 1

Body paragraph 2

Description and illustration of category 2

Body paragraph 3

Description and illustration of category 3

Concluding paragraph

■ **PRACTICE 5: Outlining an Essay**

Work with a classmate. Complete the following outline of an essay describing your friends as worrywarts, bookworms, and fatalists using the actions and activities you described in Practice 4.

Title: **My Friends**

Introduction: Why I like them all

Thesis
statement: Almost all my friends can be divided into worrywarts, bookworms, or fatalists.

Paragraph 1:   The worrywarts

What they do when they're late for something:

_____

_____

What they do when they have money trouble:

_____

_____

What they do when there's an important exam coming up:

_____

_____

Paragraph 2:   The bookworms

What they do when they're late for something:

_____

_____

What they do when they have money trouble:

_____

_____

What they do when there's an important exam coming up:

_____

_____

Paragraph 3:   The fatalists

What they do when they're late for something:

_____

_____

What they do when they have money trouble:

_____

_____

What they do when there's an important exam coming up:

_____

_____

Conclusion: In conclusion, knowing which category my friends fall into is very useful for me because I know exactly who to ask for help in every situation.

No Man Is an Island

"No man is an island, entire of itself." —John Donne, 1572–1631

Sometimes I wish that I were adopted and that I didn't know who my parents were. Then no one could say, "Your cousin Thomas gets all A's in school, so why can't you?" or "That hair of yours is just like your grandmother's; there's nothing you can do about it." The truth is that I'm not adopted, and even though I try to fight against it, I see family traits in myself all the time. The three main personality types in my family are athletic, studious, and materialistic.[1]

My father and his brother (my uncle Jonas) are athletic. They're both tall and strong. My father gets up at 5 A.M. every Sunday to drive two hours to a golf course. On weekdays, he parks his car three miles away from his office just so he can walk to work. My uncle Jonas is a terror on the basketball court. Even when he's playing with his seven-year old son, he plays to win. I know that some of that athleticism[2] has come down to me because even though I don't play sports seriously, I love working up a sweat in the gym.

The studious types in my family are the ones everybody talks about. My cousin Anna Louise, for example, is a goody-goody[3] high school student who wins many school prizes. All she knows about life is what she has read in a textbook. My brother Alfred is also studious, but he's totally different from Anna Louise. He's great with computers. He can fix anything electronic and reads all the latest electronics and science magazines. Naturally, he gets top honors in his science and math classes. I used to think that I was completely different from Anna Louise and Alfred, but now I have discovered an academic subject that I really love: history. I'm so interested in history that I carry books about history around with me everywhere I go.

My mother's two sisters and their children are the materialistic ones in our family. These two aunts have brought their kids up to believe that the only things that are valuable in the world can be counted in money. Every time I'm with these cousins, they talk about how much their new watch cost or how much money they'll make when they go into business like their dads. After two hours of that, I just have to get away. Still, I have to admit that there is a little materialist inside me as well. A friend asked to borrow my new leather coat the other day, but I said no. I had saved my money a long time to buy that coat, and I didn't want to share.

Like most people, I like to think that I am unique. However, as I get older, I can see some of the family traits in my personality. I'm not much of an athlete, but when I play tennis I'll drive myself to exhaustion rather than lose a game. Even

<table>

What about you?
What personality characteristics in your family do you share? Do you think your personality would be different if you had grown up in a different family? Share your answers with a classmate.

though I never got good grades in school, my new love of history definitely shows that I have some studious characteristics. Also, now that I am finally earning some money and have bought a few nice things, I realize that I have more in common with my irritating cousins than I used to think. Whether I like it or not, I see a little of my relatives in myself.

[1]**materialistic** *adj.* believing that money and possessions are the most important things

[2]**athleticism** *n.* being athletic

[3]**goody-goody** *n.* someone who likes to seem good when others are watching

■ **PRACTICE 6:** Analyzing Model Essay 1

With a classmate, discuss these questions about Model Essay 1.

1. What is the subject that is classified in this essay?
2. What is the classification principle?
3. How many categories does the writer divide the subject into?
4. What are the names of the categories in this essay?

Model Essay 2

May I Help You?

The world is rapidly changing from an industrial economy to a service economy. There are fewer and fewer small factories and farms. As a result, a decreasing number of people are employed in manufacturing.[1] How many shoemakers or bakers do you know? You probably don't know any, but you do know the advertising people for the shoemakers and the salespeople for oven manufacturers. In a service economy such as ours, there are service providers and consumers, who receive a service. According to the authority of the provider, there are three basic relationships between service providers and consumers: customer and salesperson, student and teacher, and patient and doctor.

In the retail[2] industry, people often say, "The customer is always right." What they mean is that a salesperson never argues with a customer. If a 350-pound man wants to buy a pink bikini swimsuit, that's his business. The salesperson is there to make the customer feel good about shopping at that particular store so that he'll come back again and again. A salesperson can try to interest the customer in a different style, but she never tells the customer what to do. In the service relationship between the customer and the salesperson, the customer has all the authority.

(continued)

The relationship between a student and a teacher is different all over the world. It also varies depending on the age of the student. We tend to accept that "the teacher is always right" through the years of compulsory[3] education. However, once people are old enough to make some choices about their education, the relationship changes. If you want to learn to play the piano, for example, you will probably look for a teacher who will teach you in the way you want to learn. Nevertheless, you still believe that your teacher knows much more about the subject than you do, so in this service relationship, the teacher has a medium level of authority.

Certain service providers have such specialized skills and knowledge that we tend to allow them complete authority in making decisions about what's best. The doctor-patient relationship is an example of such a relationship. We expect (rightly or wrongly) that the doctor is such an expert that if she says, "You need surgery," we usually don't say, "No, thank you." However, the medical profession is changing as many patients are becoming better educated about their conditions. It is now common practice in many parts of the world to get a second doctor's opinion about how to treat a serious illness. Even so, in the traditional doctor-patient relationship, it is the doctor who has most, if not all, of the authority.

In conclusion, most of us will be on both sides in a service relationship at some point in our lives. You may be a customer at noon and a salesperson at 1 P.M. You may be a teacher at age twenty-eight and a student at age fifty-eight. If you become an expert in a certain field, such as engineering, medicine, law, or psychology, you may be a client or patient one day and the service provider the next. However, you will never be both at the same time, and providing great service to your clients will still be based on the fundamental[4] principle of understanding what your customer wants and needs.

[1]**manufacturing** *n.* the process of making goods in factories	[2]**retail** *n.* the sale of goods in stores to people for their own use	[3]**compulsory** *adj.* required by law	[4]**fundamental** *adj.* basic

■ **PRACTICE 7: Analyzing Model Essay 2**

With a classmate, discuss these questions about Model Essay 2.

1. What is the subject that is classified in this essay?
2. What is the classification principle?
3. How many categories does the writer divide the subject into?
4. What are the names of the categories in this essay?

Connectors of Example and Consequence

In essays that classify, the use of connectors of example is crucial. In order for your reader to clearly grasp how you are classifying, you need to give at least one example of each category. In addition, you will frequently want to use connectors of consequence (or result) in the concluding sentence of a paragraph to summarize how your examples relate to your classification principle. Look at the chart and the model sentences that follow. Pay careful attention to the use of commas and semicolons.

CONNECTORS OF EXAMPLE AND CONSEQUENCE

	Purpose	Connectors of Example	Connectors of Consequence	Sample Sentences
Transitions	connect two independent clauses	for example for instance	as a consequence as a result consequently for this reason therefore	Some of my friends are shy. **For example,** Ching and Hiro never say much when we are with other people.
				I enjoy the peaceful company of good friends; **therefore,** I appreciate the serenity of Carlos and Maria.
Coordinating Conjunctions	connect two independent clauses		so	More and more people who live alone want a pet for company, **so** the pet services industry has expanded greatly.

■ **PRACTICE 8: Writing Sentences with Connectors**

Combine the two ideas below with a connector of example or of consequence.
Change the tense of the verb in parentheses if necessary. Watch your punctuation!

For example:

➤ sunny day—(*go*) swimming

It was a sunny day. Therefore, we went swimming.

1. miserable weather—(*cancel*) picnic

   _____

2. solar energy—(*heat*) water

   _____

3. sick—(*go*) to the doctor

   _____

4. living former U.S. presidents—(*be*) Bill Clinton

   _____

5. too much work—not (*go*) to the party

   _____

IV WRITING TO COMMUNICATE

Your Turn

Now it is your turn to write a classification essay. Choose one of the four topics below. Follow the process steps described in Appendix 1 on page 173.

Topic 1: Friends

Classify your friends. When you brainstorm, think about how you could classify your friends and what principle you could use. For example, you could classify them according to:

    a. what you do with them
    b. how you met them
    c. what you learned from them
    d. how close you feel to them
    e. when they were your friends

Now organize your essay by following this outline.

    Subject: *my friends* _____

    Principle: _____

    Category 1: _____

    Category 2: _____

    Category 3: _____

Topic 2: Movies

There are lots of ways in which you can classify movies. For example, your classification principle could be the country of origin of the movie, the way the audience reacts to the movie, whether the actors sing in the movie or not, and so on. Think of a classification principle that you are interested in and write it here:

Subject: *movies*

Principle: _____

Category 1:   _____

Category 2:   _____

Category 3:   _____

Topic 3: My Family Characteristics

Choose three kinds of traits in your family, such as appearance, interests, and skill. Write a thesis statement that includes these categories.

Consider the examples or anecdotes you will use to support your thesis statement. For example, does your category of *appearance* include only such characteristics as height, or hair color, or the shape of your nose? Or are you also going to include such characteristics as the way a person walks or sits or dresses? If you use the categories of *interests* or *skills,* you will probably want to tell a brief story (anecdote) to illustrate that category.

Subject: *my family characteristics*

Principle: _____

Category 1:   _____

Category 2:   _____

Category 3:   _____

Topic 4: Athletes

Athletes can be classified according to many principles. One principle could be how much money they earn. Another principle might be how hard or how often they play. How many other principles can you think of to classify the subject *athletes*?

Subject: *athletes*

Principle: _____

Category 1:   _____

Category 2:   _____

Category 3:   _____

Peer Help Worksheet

Trade essays and textbooks with a classmate. Read your classmate's essay while your classmate reads yours. Check off (✔) the items in your partner's book as you evaluate them. Then return the essays and books. If any of the items in your book are not checked off, and you agree with your partner, correct your essay before turning it in. Use a pencil if you write on your classmate's essay or book.

CONTENT

What did you find most interesting about this essay?

ORGANIZATION

1 This essay has _____ body paragraphs.

2 Does the thesis statement have a predictor? .... ❑

3 Does each paragraph describe one category? .... ❑

If not, write what you think the problem is:

_____

4 Does this essay have a concluding paragraph? .... ❑

5 If there is a concluding paragraph, which of these components does it have? (Check all that apply.)

- a restatement .... ❑
- a summary .... ❑
- a final comment .... ❑

MECHANICS

1 How many of the following connectors are there in this essay?

(Write the number in the blank.)

_____ connectors of example

_____ connectors of consequence

2 Do you think commas and semicolons are used correctly with each of these? .... ❑

If not, discuss any possible mistakes with the writer.

Writing to Communicate . . . More

Look around you. Almost anything can be classified: trees, animals, chemicals, theories of government, and so on. Here are some other topics that lend themselves to a classification organizational pattern. Choose one and write an essay about it. Refer to Appendix 1 to review the writing process before you write.

1. Some people like to have cats as pets, some people prefer snakes, and other people can't stand pets at all. Think about how you can classify people according to the kinds of pets they like.

2. The number of jobs people can have seems endless, but many jobs have common features. Classify the subject *jobs* into a manageable number of categories—no more than five or six. Write an essay that classifies these jobs.

3. All countries have a political system of organization; however, they also differ in the way their governments are set up. Using the classification principle of *political system,* write an essay that explains your classification.

Relationships in Cyberspace

I VOCABULARY BUILDER

A. *How much do you know about cyberspace? Work with a classmate to match the word with its definition. Then change the word form in the e-mail below if necessary.*

_____ **1.** emoticon

_____ **2.** instant messaging (IM)

_____ **3.** chat

_____ **4.** spam

_____ **5.** surf

_____ **6.** wireless

a. junk e-mail; e-mail you don't want from someone you don't know

b. real-time communication in writing between two people

c. use the Internet to look for information

d. a symbol for feelings; for example, ☺

e. Internet connection without a cable

f. real-time communication in writing among more than two people

B. *Use the words from Part A to fill in the blanks of the e-mail.*

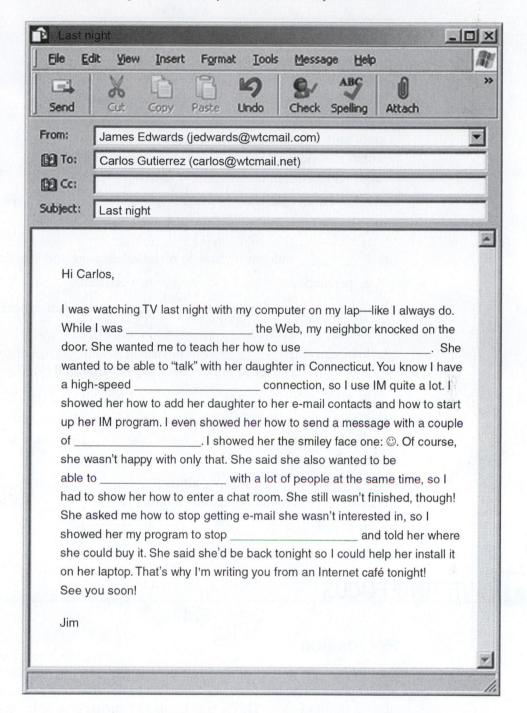

Last night — ☐ ☐ ☒

File Edit View Insert Format Tools Message Help

Send Cut Copy Paste Undo Check Spelling Attach

From: James Edwards (jedwards@wtcmail.com)

To: Carlos Gutierrez (carlos@wtcmail.net)

Cc:

Subject: Last night

Hi Carlos,

I was watching TV last night with my computer on my lap—like I always do. While I was _____ the Web, my neighbor knocked on the door. She wanted me to teach her how to use _____. She wanted to be able to "talk" with her daughter in Connecticut. You know I have a high-speed _____ connection, so I use IM quite a lot. I showed her how to add her daughter to her e-mail contacts and how to start up her IM program. I even showed her how to send a message with a couple of _____. I showed her the smiley face one: ☺. Of course, she wasn't happy with only that. She said she also wanted to be able to _____ with a lot of people at the same time, so I had to show her how to enter a chat room. She still wasn't finished, though! She asked me how to stop getting e-mail she wasn't interested in, so I showed her my program to stop _____ and told her where she could buy it. She said she'd be back tonight so I could help her install it on her laptop. That's why I'm writing you from an Internet café tonight! See you soon!

Jim

C. Study the verbs below. Then, cricle the correct verb to complete each sentence.

> **convince** *v.* to make someone believe in something
>
> **emerge** *v.* to appear; to begin
>
> **expand** *v.* to grow bigger
>
> **overwhelm** *v.* to present with an excessive amount
>
> **persist** *v.* to hold firmly to a purpose
>
> **persuade** *v.* to make someone do something
>
> **scroll** *v.* to move up and down a computer screen
>
> **urge** *v.* to encourage someone to do something

1. I _____ in learning how to make a Web page and was finally successful.

   a. persuaded   **b.** persisted

2. I'm _____ with work this week. Can we have lunch next week instead?

   a. overwhelmed   **b.** urged

3. Joan, can you _____ your boyfriend to help me install an anti-virus program? I get a lot of junk e-mail, and I'm afraid I'll get a computer virus.

   a. scroll   **b.** persuade

4. I'm _____ that I need to get a new Internet Service Provider (ISP). What do you think?

   a. convinced   **b.** expanded

5. He _____ me to stop sending him e-mail to his office account. He said that his boss might see it and wouldn't like it.

   a. urged   **b.** emerged

II WRITING FOCUS

Persuasion

Persuasion gets to the heart of academic writing. In a sense, the purpose of all academic writing is to persuade someone to do something or to convince someone of your point of view. This is why thesis statements give opinions. In a persuasive essay, as in all essays, the body paragraphs explain your **arguments** or reasons why you think the way you do.

Choosing a Topic for a Persuasive Essay

People can disagree about anything. They can disagree about how many cell phones were sold last year, who the president of South Africa is, or what the best kind of coffee is. However, none of these topics will make a good persuasive essay. The first two topics are about facts, and statements about facts are either right or wrong. The last topic deals with a matter of taste and personal belief, and persuasive arguments do not change your personal tastes or your beliefs.

When you write a persuasive essay, it's important to choose a topic that can be influenced by persuasive arguments. In addition, you must have an opinion about this issue and state it. Arguments about legal topics are good examples. Should we allow sixteen-year-olds to drive cars? If yes, why? If no, why not? Should we permit tobacco or alcohol sales in our state? Why or why not? If you can't see two sides to an issue, then it probably won't make a good persuasive essay.

■ *PRACTICE 1:* **Determining What Makes a Good Topic for a Persuasive Essay**

Below are six possible topics for persuasive essays. For each topic: Decide whether you think each topic will make a good persuasive essay. Put a check mark (✓) in the column of your choice. Discuss your choices with a classmate.

Topics	good persuasive essay topic	poor persuasive essay topic; it's about facts	poor persuasive essay topic; it's a matter of taste or personal belief
types of new cars			
the uses of technology			
the value of technology			
the best place to go on vacation			
the use of animals in medical testing			
the worst accident I ever had			
the most delicious flavor			

Ordering of Arguments

When you consider your arguments for a particular thesis statement you want to support, you need to decide the order in which you want to present your ideas to the reader. These are the main organizational patterns:

● **Ascending order** means starting with the least important and building up to your strongest argument.

● **Equal order** means that you feel that all your arguments are of equal importance, so the order in which you place your arguments isn't important.

The most common type of order used in persuasive essays is ascending order because most writers want the reader to remember what the strongest argument is.

Graphic Organizers

Introductory paragraph

Thesis statement

Body paragraph 1

Your least important argument and support for that argument

Body paragraph 2

Your second most important argument and support for that argument

Body paragraph 3

Your most important argument and support for that argument

Concluding paragraph

Equal Order

Introductory paragraph

Thesis statement

Body paragraph 1

Your first argument and support for that argument

Body paragraph 2

Your second argument and support for that argument

Body paragraph 3

Your third argument and support for that argument

Concluding paragraph

■ PRACTICE 2: Ordering Arguments

Below you will find a thesis statement and three arguments to support it. With a classmate, discuss which of these arguments are more or less important. Put number 1 in front of the argument you think is most important, 2 in front of the second most important, and 3 in front of the least important argument. Then explain to the class why you ordered the arguments in this way.

Thesis statement: *Electronic communication is hurting students' writing skills.*

Arguments:

_____ Because they depend on the spell checker, students aren't learning how to spell.

_____ Students use the same casual style in their school papers as in their e-mails.

_____ Students use abbreviations and emoticons even in their academic essays.

■ PRACTICE 3: Practicing Argumentation

Below are two thesis statements. With one or two classmates, discuss arguments that you can give to support each thesis statement. Then order them.

1. Electronic communication is very useful for senior citizens.

    a. _____

    b. _____

    c. _____

2. Electronic communication is good for the environment.

    a. _____

    b. _____

    c. _____

Model Essay 1

Everyone Is Talking, and No One Is Listening

Since the middle of the 1990s, the ability to communicate electronically has expanded dramatically. Electronic communication is changing how people relate to one another. However, one thing remains constant: These new forms of communication are not face to face. They are distant, and they keep people at a distance. In my opinion, due to electronic communication, relationships today are changing for the worse; they have become fragmented,[1] superficial,[2] and anonymous.[3]

(continued)

Communication these days is becoming a process of exchanging messages of two or three words. There is no longer time for serious and deep reflection. For example, in most countries, sending a text message via a cell phone is much cheaper than talking on that phone, so people send each other silly messages like "RU ready?" or "4 sure." The language of Shakespeare and Milton has become reduced to abbreviations. With Instant Messenger (IM), people send each other emoticons such as a smiley face instead of sentences. In addition, since Instant Messenger depends on who has the fastest connection, there cannot be real communication. There is no give-and-take. These fragmented messages are not true communication.

The current ability to relate to one another electronically is largely textual; that is, people read messages from each other. Blogs, or Web logs, have become the way to communicate. However, anyone, anywhere can create a blog, and they can write anything they want. There are millions of blogs being produced. It seems that everyone wants to shout, "Hey, here I am! This is me!", but no one really listens. No one responds. Another reason why relationships are becoming more superficial is the spread of e-mail. It's impossible to have a serious discussion with people through e-mail. Because they are overwhelmed by spam in addition to real messages, people just skim what they see and either make a rapid, thoughtless response or ignore it completely. No one reads e-mail messages carefully because there are just too many of them.

Finally, while one great advantage of the World Wide Web is that it is anonymous, this is also its major disadvantage. Anyone can pretend to be anyone. For example, a sixteen-year-old high school student could say that he is a twenty three-year-old college graduate, and the person reading his blog or profile would never know. This type of anonymity can also put Internet users at risk. There are many news stories about a criminal convincing a teenager to meet him at a coffee shop or a mall. The teenager agrees to meet her Internet friend because she thinks she is meeting another teenager. The Web knows no one; a person can invent an identity. It's clear that there can be no real communication when it's so easy for someone to remain anonymous.

In short, electronic communication has multiple advantages, but it also has disadvantages. This new form of communication makes people lonelier because they don't make real and meaningful connections. The communication is fragmented and superficial, and it is not always honest because of the ability to be anonymous. Fewer silly messages and more face-to-face communication would make us better people, I think.

[1]**fragmented** adj. separated into many parts; not seeming to have a main purpose	[2]**superficial** adj. trivial and unimportant	[3]**anonymous** adj. giving a false name or no name at all

■ PRACTICE 4: Analyzing Model Essay 1

With a classmate, discuss the answers to the following questions.

1. Which organizational pattern does this essay follow? (Check one.)

   ❏ ascending order   ❏ equal order

2. What is the predictor in the thesis statement?

3. The first body paragraph supports the opinion that electronic communication has made our relationships more fragmented. Give an example of each of the communication methods the author mentions:

   a. Abbreviations: _____

   b. Emoticons: _____

4. How do the author's examples of blogs and the increase of e-mail support the second opinion that electronic communication is superficial? Give two examples.

   a. _____

   b. _____

5. Give two examples in the essay to support the author's third argument that electronic communication makes people anonymous.

   a. _____

   b. _____

6. Do you think this essay is convincing? Why or why not?

   _____

   _____

Model Essay 2

Dating in Cyberspace

The number of single people in the United States has been increasing for several years. Many of them like being single and do not want to find a marriage partner. Some, however, want to find someone, but they're too busy to spend the time. They don't want to invest time in a relationship, find out that they aren't compatible, and have to start all over again. There is a solution to this problem: cyberdating. Anyone who is seriously looking for a partner should try cyberdating.

(continued)

For one thing, cyberdating is extremely convenient. There are many reputable[1] websites that make it easy to post your profile[2] for others to see. Once you have posted your profile, you read about the thousands of others who have done the same. You can take as much or as little time as you like looking through the database. Also, these sites are available twenty-four hours a day, so you can search when you have the time.

Furthermore, cyberdating can keep you from being hurt. Too often on a first date, you see boredom or disappointment in your date's eyes. All you can do in this situation is to persevere[3] and hope the date ends early. With cyberdating, however, the people you decide to meet have already seen a photo of you, and they already know a lot about you. There is no surprise, so there is no disappointment. In fact, it's just the opposite. You and your date are excited to meet each other, and you look at each other with hope.

Finally, the anxiety[4] of dating is greatly lessened with cyberdating. Traditionally, men take the lead in dating. They are the ones who have to ask a woman out on a date. They have to risk rejection.[5] It's no better for women, however. Many women still wait for a man to ask them out first. Then, if they don't want to go out with him, they have to let the man down gently. While it's true that sometimes with cyberdating men still get rejected and women still reject, you experience this in the privacy of your own home. Moreover, you never have to see the person again because you have never met! It's the perfect solution.

In short, if you are looking for someone to date and even marry, you should go online and post your profile on a dating website. It's convenient, safe, and worry-free.

---

[1] **reputable** *adj.* respected for being honest and doing good work

[2] **profile** *n.* a short description that gives important details about someone or something

[3] **persevere** *v.* to continue trying to do something difficult in a determined way

[4] **anxiety** *n.* strong feelings of worry about something

[5] **rejection** *n.* the act of not accepting something

■ PRACTICE 5: Analyzing Model Essay 2

With a classmate, discuss the answers to these questions about Model Essay 2.

1. Which organizational pattern does this essay follow? (Check one.)

   ❑ ascending order   ❑ equal order

2. What is the thesis statement? Does it have a predictor? If so, what is it?

3. Does each of the body paragraphs have a clear topic sentence? Underline the topic sentences.

4. Are the topic sentences necessary? Why or why not?

5. What are the arguments that the author gives to try to convince the reader of the value of cyberdating?

6. Do you think this essay is convincing? Why or why not?

III STRUCTURE AND MECHANICS

Connectors of Argumentation

As you know, connectors are useful in showing relationships between ideas in your writing. The connectors commonly used in persuasive essays are transitions. Some transitions order your arguments as ascending or equal. Others are used to strengthen an argument. Look at this chart and study the sample sentences.

Connectors for Argumentation				
	Purpose	**Adding Strength**	**Most Important**	**Sample Sentences**
Transition	*connect two independent clauses*	indeed in fact	most importantly most significantly above all most of all	When I'm away on business, e-mail allows me to communicate with my wife every day. **Indeed**, we seem to communicate best through e-mail. There are many things to remember when you write a research paper on the computer. **Above all**, you must save your document frequently so that you don't lose any work.
	Purpose	**Equal**	**Final**	**Sample Sentence**
Transition	*connect two independent clauses*	equally important for one thing for another thing	finally lastly	There are many reasons to have several e-mail accounts; **for one thing**, you can keep your social life and your professional life separate.

PRACTICE 6: Using Connectors of Argumentation

Use one of the transitions in the chart on page 151 to fill in each blank below. More than one answer is possible. After you finish, share your completed paragraph with a classmate or a small group.

> **Pre-Internet Life**
>
> Life before the Internet was much better. _____, going to your mailbox was more interesting. _____, you might find an actual personal letter. _____, libraries were used more. _____, people visited or called each other more often instead of just e-mailing them. Nowadays, no one needs to leave the house to find information. In short, people were better off before the Internet changed everything.

IV WRITING TO COMMUNICATE

Your Turn

Write an argumentation essay about electronic communication.

1. First consider: What is your opinion of electronic communication? Narrow down your topic to one specific type of electronic communication and/or to one specific problem or benefit.

2. Next, consider a possible thesis statement for your essay. Write the first draft here: _____

_____

Now brainstorm with your classmates some ideas that support this thesis statement. You may choose to use a mind map. Write your thesis in the center of the circle below and draw lines in all directions with your arguments and reasons (see below).

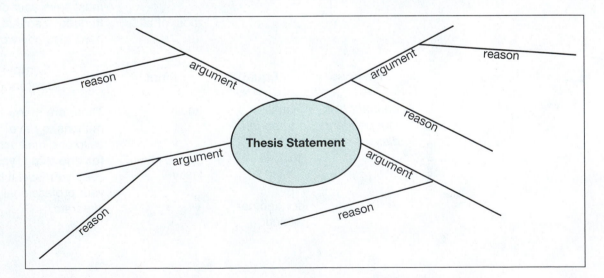

Peer Help Worksheet

Trade essays and textbooks with a classmate. Read your classmate's essay while your classmate reads yours. Check off (✓) the items in your partner's book as you evaluate them. Then return the essays and books. If any of the items in your book are not checked off, and you agree with your partner, correct your essay before turning it in. Use a pencil if you write on your classmate's essay or book.

CONTENT

1 What did you particularly like about this essay?

2 Does the essay convince you? Why or why not?

ORGANIZATION

1 Does the thesis statement in this essay have a predictor? . . . . . ❏

2 Do the body paragraphs support the thesis statement? . . . . ❏

3 Which type of introductory paragraph does the essay contain? (Check one.)

    a. anecdote . . . . ❏

    b. historical . . . . ❏

    c. general to specific . . . . ❏

4 Which ordering of body paragraphs is used? (Check one.)

    a. ascending . . . . ❏

    b. equal . . . . ❏

5 Which components does the concluding paragraph contain? (Check all that apply.)

    a. a summary . . . . ❏

    b. a restatement of the thesis statement . . . . ❏

    c. a final comment . . . . ❏

MECHANICS

1 There are ____ connectors or argumentation. (Write the number.)

2 Do you think they are used correctly? . . . . ❏

    If not, discuss any possible mistakes with the writer.

Writing to Communicate . . . More

Below are three other topics for a persuasive essay about electronic communication. Refer to Appendix 1 to review the writing process before you write.

1. Online education is *as good as / better than / worse than* education in a classroom.
2. Making friends on the Web is *dangerous / not realistic / better than* trying to meet people face to face.
3. Online newspapers are *better / worse* than paper newspapers.

Urban Lifestyles

I VOCABULARY BUILDER

A. *Read this poem out loud to a classmate and try to imagine the sound that the verbs describe in each line. Then write five of the verbs from the poem in the sentences below.*

The Sounds of the City

Horns honk

Brakes screech

Doors slam

Children scream

TVs hum

Voices shout

Church bells ring

And the winter's first snow covers all in its blanket of peace.

1. My new dishwasher is great. While the old dishwasher used to screech, my new one just _____.

2. Whenever my friend drives by my house, he _____ his horn to say hello.

(continued)

3. On our campus, we have a clock tower whose bells _____ every day at noon.

4. He left in anger and _____ the garden gate shut behind him.

5. When the doctor set his broken arm, the man _____ in pain.

B. *The photos below are of the J. Paul Getty Museum in Los Angeles ("The Getty") and the Metropolitan Museum of Art in New York ("The Met"). The adjectives in the box on page 157 can be used to describe the two buildings. Which ones do you think describe the Getty and which ones describe the Met? Write the words in the chart.*

The J. Paul Getty Museum

The Metropolitan Museum of Art

| angular | classical | modern | plain | rounded |
| asymmetrical | curvy | ornate | rectangular | symmetrical |

Adjectives describing the Getty	Adjectives describing the Met

C. *Look at the pictures of the two museums again and discuss with your classmates five ways to describe the differences between the buildings. Use the adjectives in the chart above.*

1. Unlike the Getty, the Met is _____.

2. The buildings are different in that the Getty is _____, while the Met is _____.

3. The shape of the Met is _____, but the Getty has a(n) _____ shape.

4. The Met looks _____. On the other hand, the Getty is _____.

5. The Getty is _____, whereas the Met is more _____.

Comparing and Contrasting

Comparing and **contrasting** are very common in academic writing. The purpose of a comparison is to show how people, places, things, or ideas are similar, and the purpose of contrast is to show how people, places, things, or ideas are different. For example, in a computer science class, you may be asked to compare two programming languages. In a literature class, your instructor may ask you to compare two novels. In a political science class, your assignment may be to contrast two or more theories of economics.

Graphic Organizers

There are basically three ways of organizing essays that compare and contrast. They are called **basic block**, **block comparison**, and **point-by-point comparison**.

Basic Block Style

The first style first introduces the similarities between two objects and then the differences, or vice versa. It looks like this:

Introductory paragraph
Thesis statement

Body paragraph 1
Similarities between A and B

Body paragraph 2
Differences between A and B

Concluding paragraph

Block Comparison Style

The second style also has two body paragraphs. However, this style describes one item only in the first body paragraph and describes a second item in the second body paragraph. The second body paragraph shows how the second item compares with the first one by using the same categories of comparison. This style looks like this:

Introductory paragraph
Thesis statement

Body paragraph 1
Points about A
1
2
3

Body paragraph 2
Points about B in comparison to A
1
2
3

Concluding paragraph

Point-by-Point Comparison Style

The third style is a comparison-and-contrast essay. This style has several body paragraphs, and there are as many body paragraphs as there are points of comparison.

Introductory paragraph
Thesis statement

Body paragraph 1
Point 1: A and B

Body paragraph 2
Point 2: A and B

Body paragraph 3
Point 3: A and B

Concluding paragraph

The Getty and the Met

There are countless art museums in the United States. Some are small and consist of a single room, and others cover city blocks. Two of them, the Metropolitan Museum of Art in New York and the J. Paul Getty Museum in Los Angeles, are visited every day by tourists as well as locals. While these two museums have similarities because they are both places that exhibit art, I believe their differences are more striking than their similarities.

Both the Met, as the Metropolitan Museum of Art is known, and the Getty have amazing collections of art. The art spans[1] many centuries, from antiquity[2] to modern times. They are both enormously popular. The Met has thousands of visitors every day; likewise, the Getty is so popular that there is often a waiting list just to get in. Both have been used as movie locations, and the citizens of New York and Los Angeles are proud of their famous museums.

However, in three distinct ways, the Met and the Getty are almost opposites. First of all, their architecture is very different. The architectural style of the Met is classical, ornate, and symmetrical. The Getty, in contrast, is modern, plain, and asymmetrical. They also vary a lot in age. The construction of the Met was begun in 1880 and completed in 1902, and it is now well over 100 years old. The Getty, on the other hand, was just completed in 1997. Finally, the relationship between the buildings and the art inside is quite different in the two museums. While the architecture of the Met is impressive, the real treasure of the museum lies inside its walls in its fantastic collections. The Getty, in contrast, was designed and constructed as an impressive organization of walls and spaces. In fact, I believe that more people spend time outside enjoying the gardens, trees, and the exterior atmosphere of the Getty than ever go inside.

In conclusion, these two museums do have several similarities, but I feel strongly that their differences outnumber the ways in which they are similar. In their architecture, their locations, and their relationship to the art they display, the two museums are worlds apart.

What about you?

Are there museums in the town in which you grew up? Describe one of them to your classmate.

---

[1] **span** *v.* to include all of a period of time

[2] **antiquity** *n.* the period from the fifth century BCE until the seventh century CE

■ **PRACTICE 1:** Analyzing Model Essay 1

With a classmate, discuss the following questions and then write the answers.

1. What is being compared in this essay? _____

2. What is the organizational style of this essay? Check (✔) the style that applies.
   ❑ Basic block
   ❑ Block comparison
   ❑ Point-by-point comparison

3. What are the topics of the two body paragraphs of this essay?
   Paragraph 1: _____
   Paragraph 2: _____

4. What are the similarities the author mentions?
   _____
   _____

5. What are the differences the author mentions?
   _____
   _____

Model Essay 2

A Tale[1] of Two Towns

"Where do you come from?" is a question many Americans can't answer easily. Many Americans were born in one place, lived a few years in another, went to elementary school in a third town, and so on. In my home country, Norway, people usually live all their lives in the town where they were born, but my family is different. We moved from one small town to another when I was twelve years old. For this reason, I have two "hometowns." Although the people in these two towns, Kristiansand and Arendal, think that they have nothing in common,[2] in my opinion, they have far more similarities than differences.

The first obvious similarity lies in the location of the two towns. They are both seaside towns on the south coast of Norway. They are sheltered from the ocean storms by a large group of islands and backed by hills that defend them against the cold winter winds. There are a few minor differences in their location, of course: Kristiansand, my childhood city, has now grown to include neighborhoods across the many islands between it and the ocean, while in Arendal, my teenage town, those islands are still largely unpopulated.

Second, both Kristiansand and Arendal are small. Compared to the great continental cities of Paris and Rome, they are not even dots on a map. Kristiansand is larger with about 76,000 inhabitants, while Arendal has only about 35,000, but neither can be called a metropolis.[3]

(continued)

Furthermore, at least to a visitor, they are quite similar in their natural beauty. The islands are rough and rocky. The houses of both towns are mostly small, white-painted wooden buildings, and almost exactly the same kinds of plants and trees grow in both places. In addition, the ocean is a major influence on the lifestyle of both towns, and the weather forecast is the major topic of conversation.

The economies of the two towns are also based on the same business: tourism. Both native Norwegians and foreigners go on summer vacation to the two towns, and in winter, business is very slow. Of course, there are a few differences here as well. In Arendal, there are still quite a lot of fishermen making a living[4] from the sea, while Kristiansand is a busy port[5] for large commercial ships. Still, I doubt that either town could support its population without the tourists.

Finally, despite the opinions of the natives of Kristiansand and Arendal, I think that the people there are very similar. Because of the size of the towns, people are mostly interested in what their neighbors do and say, and they don't care very much about what is happening in the outside world. In addition, the inhabitants of the two towns have a love/hate relationship with the necessary tourists. These tourists bring in business and money in the summer, so the natives smile at them when they meet them. However, behind their backs, the townspeople wish that the tourists would just spend their money and go home.

Thus, while there are a few differences between Arendal and Kristiansand, I think that the similarities are far more obvious. In location, size, natural beauty, economy, and people, they are very much alike. Although I sometimes feel they are too small for me now, they are my hometowns, and there is no place like home.

What about you?

Think about two cities you know. What are the first points of comparison that come to mind? Their locations, cultural attractions, or shopping districts, or something else? What are other ways to compare these two cities? Share your thoughts with a classmate.

[1]**tale** *n.* a story
[2]**have nothing in common** *idiom* to be very different from each other
[3]**metropolis** *n.* a very large city
[4]**make a living from** *idiom* to get their income from
[5]**port** *n.* a place where ships can load and unload people or things

■ PRACTICE 2: Analyzing Model Essay 2

With a classmate, discuss these questions and then write the answers.

1. What is being compared in this essay? _____

2. What is the organizational style of this essay? Check (✔) the style that applies.
   ❑ Basic block
   ❑ Block comparison
   ❑ Point-by-point comparison

3. What are the topics of the five body paragraphs of this essay?

Paragraph 1: _____

Paragraph 2: _____

Paragraph 3: _____

Paragraph 4: _____

Paragraph 5: _____

4. How many differences are there? How many similarities?

Differences: _____   Similarities: _____

Model Essay 3

East Side Story

It seems that every village, town, and city worldwide has its richer and poorer neighborhoods. In the United States, the poor area is called the "wrong side of the tracks." "Tracks" comes from the railroad tracks that used to divide a town, but, of course, anything can divide a city. In the city where I grew up, a river divides the town into the west side and the east side. The west side is the rich side of the city, and the east side is the poor area. Not surprisingly, life is a lot easier on the west side of town than it is on the east side of town.

In the west, there are lots of parks and open spaces. This part of town has wide streets with plenty of parking and many wonderful shops that charge enormous prices for a simple T-shirt. In addition, you always feel completely safe on the west side of town. Not only are there plenty of police officers, but also the lights and crowds of people make you feel safe. In spite of all these people, the west side is amazingly quiet. You hear people chatting[1] in sidewalk cafes and maybe a car's horn, but, in general, the west side has a pleasing calm. Life feels good on the west side of town.

The east side of the river, on the other hand, contrasts with the west in almost every way. There are practically no parks on the east side. The entire area is made up of building after building. A tree would not survive; every square foot is covered with asphalt.[2] Moreover, the people who live on the east side do not have easy access[3] to shopping. When they want to buy food, they have to travel a long way to find a good grocery store, or they must settle for the small selection at a tiny local market. Third, you always have to be a little careful on the east side. It's true that there are police officers there, but they are almost always busy doing something else and not really paying attention. It's not completely safe. Finally, the east side is not quiet. Doors slam in the apartment buildings. The brakes on the streetcars screech. In addition, people shout a lot more on the east side than they do on the west side of the river.

(continued)

To sum it all up, it's a lot easier to live on the west side than on the east. However, as the old saying goes, "Money can't buy happiness." The westsiders have money, big houses, beautiful parks, convenient shopping, security, and quiet. To us eastsiders, though, their lives are boring. With our buildings and bustling[4] city streets, our family-owned local markets, our exciting urban action, and our constant noise of people and traffic, ours is the better life. I was born on the wrong side of the tracks, and I'll never move.

What about you?

Is there a part of your hometown that is the "wrong side of the tracks"? How is it different from other parts of town? Share your thoughts with a classmate.

[1]**chat** *v.* to talk in a friendly and informal way

[2]**asphalt** *n.* a hard black substance used on the surface of roads

[3]**access** *n.* the right to enter into a place

[4]**bustling** *adj.* busy and loud

■ PRACTICE 3: **Analyzing Model Essay 3**

With a classmate, discuss the following questions and then write the answers.

1. What is being compared in this essay? _____

2. What is the organizational style of this essay? Check (✔) the style that applies.
   ❑ Basic block
   ❑ Block comparison
   ❑ Point-by-point comparison

3. What are the topics of the two body paragraphs of this essay?
   Paragraph 1: _____
   Paragraph 2: _____

4. List the points of comparison between the neighborhoods as they are described in this essay.

   _____   _____

   _____   _____

   _____   _____

Connectors of Comparison and Contrast

There are four types of connectors of comparison and contrast: **transitions**, **coordinating conjunctions**, **subordinating conjunctions**, and **prepositions**.

Connectors of Comparison

Look at the following chart containing the most common comparison connectors and study the sample sentences, which compare two imaginary towns, Stonecreek and Linden.

		Purpose	Comparison	Sample Sentences
	Transitions	*connect two independent clauses*	likewise similarly	Linden has a town hall built in 1891. Stonecreek, **similarly**, has a town hall built at the end of the nineteenth century.
Conjunctions	Subordinate	*introduce adverb clauses*		
	Coordinate	*connect two nouns or independent clauses*	both . . . and neither . . . nor not only . . . but also	**Both** Stonecreek **and** Linden have much to offer tourists. **Neither** Stonecreek **nor** Linden has a population problem. **Not only** do stores sell a lot in Linden, **but** they **also** sell a lot in Stonecreek.
	Prepositions	*precede nouns or noun phrases*	like similar to	Stonecreek's town hall is **like** Linden's.

Connectors of Contrast

There are two ways to make a contrast: to say two things are different, and to say that two things are opposites. The first one is called a **simple contrast**, and the second one is called a **direct contrast**. Look at the following chart containing the most common connectors of both types of contrast. Study the sample sentences, which contrast Stonecreek and Linden.

Connectors of Contrast				
	Purpose	Simple Contrast	Direct Contrast	Sample Sentences
Transitions	connect two independent clauses	in contrast however	on the other hand however	Linden's population is mostly German; **in contrast,** Stonecreek's population is very mixed. Linden is exciting. **On the other hand,** Stonecreek is quiet.
Conjunctions — Subordinate	introduce adverb clauses		while whereas	Stonecreek is small, **whereas** Linden is large. **While** Stonecreek is small, Linden is large.
Conjunctions — Coordinate	connect two independent clauses	but yet	but yet	Stonecreek is in a valley, **but** Linden is on the coast. Linden is large, **yet** Stonecreek is small.
Prepositions	precede nouns or noun phrases	in contrast to different from	unlike	**In contrast to** Stonecreek's harsh winters, Linden's winters are mild. **Unlike** Stonecreek, Linden has many traffic problems.

■ PRACTICE 4: Selecting Connectors

Choose the best connectors to complete the paragraph by circling one of the choices in bold. Use the punctuation marks and sentence structure to help you select the appropriate expression.

Life in High-Rise Apartments

Even though they have similarities, I think it's better to live on the top floors of a high-rise building than it is to live on the lower floors. One similarity is that (**both / not only**) the top floors (**and / but also**) the lower floors have the same types and sizes of apartments. In addition, renters on the top floor are (**unlike / similar to**) renters on the bottom floors in that they deal with the same owner and staff. (**Likewise / However**), there are reasons to prefer the top floors. The top  floors are quiet (**whereas / in contrast to**) the noisy lower floors. Also, the views are better. On the top floors, you can see the entire city. (**Different from / On the other hand**), the view on the lower floor is of buildings, cars, and people. Finally, (**unlike / likewise**) top floor apartments, the sun never shines on the lower floors because there are too many tall buildings around. In conclusion, I prefer living on the top floors of a high-rise to living on the lower floors.

■ **PRACTICE 5:** Writing Sentences Using Connectors of Comparison or Contrast

David studies at the University of Colorado in Boulder. He's trying to decide whether to buy a used car or take the bus. He needs to get to his classes at different times; sometimes a class begins at eight o'clock in the morning, and other days his classes end at ten at night. He also loves to go mountain climbing and hiking in the mountains outside Boulder. Below, David has written a list of the differences between buying and driving a car and taking the bus.

On a separate piece of paper, make complete sentences from the ideas listed for each point of comparison and connect them with connectors from the charts on pages 165 and 166. You may not need to use all the words in every sentence.

Point of Comparison	Buy and Drive a Car	Take the Bus
Convenience	Car parked outside the house	Walk to the bus stop
Speed	Can drive directly to destination	Bus makes many stops
Cost	Car = $5,000 Insurance = $100 / month Gas = $40 / month Parking = $50 / month	Bus pass is free for university students
Weather	Dangerous to drive in snowstorms	Bus is safe because of better equipment
Get out of town	Easy and fast to get to the mountains	Need to take three buses to get to the mountains

Your Turn

Write a comparison and/or contrast essay on one of the topics below. It should be about three or four pages, typed, and submitted as an attachment to an e-mail no later than _____.

Analyze the assignment to be sure you understand it.

Brainstorm one of the topics below.

1. My Hometown Then and Now

   Your hometown has certainly changed over the years. How is it different now? Are the houses different? The systems of transportation, the number of people, the crime rate, the parks and other natural spaces? Are there more jobs and opportunities than before?

2. Two Great Cities

   What are your favorite cities? You may think about cities you know well or ones you have only read about. What is exciting or enjoyable about these cities?

3. Urban and Rural Living

   What are some differences between living in an urban area and living in a rural area? For example, consider the types of buildings, the types of activities, the types of jobs, the environment, and the lifestyles.

Organize your ideas by going through the following steps:

1. Ask yourself: Do the differences outweigh the similarities of the two topics, or do the similarities outweigh the differences?

2. Write your thesis statement.

3. Decide which pattern of organization (basic block, block comparison, or point-by-point) would be best for the topic.

4. Write an outline.

Write the first draft of your essay following your outline. Write the body paragraphs first. Then think of an interesting anecdote for your introductory paragraph. Finally, write your concluding paragraph by restating the thesis statement, summarizing the main points of your essay, and/or making a final comment.

Rewrite your draft by exchanging your essay with a classmate. Use the Peer Help Worksheet on page 169 to help each other improve your essays.

Write the final paper (or next draft) of your essay.

Peer Help Worksheet

Trade essays and textbooks with a classmate. Read your classmate's essay while your classmate reads yours. Check off (✔) the items in your partner's book as you evaluate them. Then return the essays and books. If any of the items in your book are not checked off, and you agree with your partner, correct your essay before turning it in. Use a pencil if you write on your classmate's essay or book.

CONTENT

1 What did you particularly like about this essay?

2 What does the essay mostly describe? (Check one.)

   a. differences . . . . ❑

   b. similarities . . . . ❑

3 Do you think the essay could be improved by adding more
or different examples? . . . . ❑

   If so, what would you suggest to the writer?

ORGANIZATION

1 There are _____ body paragraphs in this essay. (Write the number.)

2 What kind of organization is used? (Check one.)

   a. basic block . . . . ❑

   b. block comparison. . . . . ❑

   c. point-by-point. . . . . ❑

   d. it's unclear . . . . ❑

MECHANICS

1 There are _____ connectors in this essay. (Write the number.)

2 Do you think the punctuation for each connector is correct? . . . . ❑

   If not, discuss any possible mistakes with the writer.

Writing to Communicate . . . More

Here are some other topics that lend themselves to a comparison-and-contrast organizational pattern. Choose one and write an essay about it. Refer to Appendix 1 to review the writing process before you write.

1. Your parents probably led quite different lives when they were young than you do now. Write an essay comparing your lifestyle with your mother's or father's.

2. Think about a movie you have seen that was based on a book you have read. Compare and/or contrast the book and the movie.

3. Compare the customary food in two different cities.

BRINGING IT ALL TOGETHER

I REVIEWING IDEAS

A. *Each topic below lends itself to a particular rhetorical pattern. Check (✔) the box of the pattern you would use for each. Explain your choice to a classmate. Note that some topics could be developed in more than one way.*

Topic	Process	Classification	Persuasion	Comparison/contrast
A governmental policy				
Musical instruments				
How to conduct an experiment				
The sounds of the city				
Salt water vs. fresh water				
A new law				
Two movies				
Getting a new pet				

B. *Read the introductory paragraph below and the pieces of support that follow it. As you read, decide what ideas from the list support each body paragraph by completing the outline. Note that some ideas are irrelevant and shouldn't go in any paragraph. Then discuss your choices with a classmate.*

Counting People

The earliest known census, or counting of people in a certain area, took place in Persia (present-day Iran) about 2,500 years ago. The government wanted information about the number of people in order to levy taxes. Since then, governments around the world take censuses for this and many other reasons. In the United States, a census is taken every ten years, and its results have consequences in education, business, and politics.

Possible support for paragraphs

1. how many students go to a school
2. how to advertise products
3. what children learn
4. when people go shopping
5. where a political district is
6. where people vote
7. how much money schools get
8. where to advertise products

Body paragraph 1
Topic: _____
Supports: _____

Body paragraph 2
Topic: _____
Supports: _____

Body paragraph 3
Topic: _____
Supports: _____

*Write **C** (Correct) in the blank if the sentence has no punctuation mistakes. Write **I** (Incorrect) if the sentence has a mistake. Fix the incorrect sentences by adding or deleting commas, semicolons, periods, or capital letters. Then compare your corrections with a classmate.*

—— **1.** José Luis is outgoing; whereas, his wife is very shy.

—— **2.** Yoga instructors use many techniques. For example, they instruct their students in breathing, stretching, chanting, and meditating.

—— **3.** The computer technician exhorted me to back up my files but I didn't listen and lost some documents.

—— **4.** The brakes on my car are screeching again, therefore; I have to take the car to the mechanic.

—— **5.** Even though her doctor told her to get more aerobic exercise, Bella rarely walks more than a few yards at a time.

—— **6.** Francis is a reckless driver so his parents took his license away.

—— **7.** I love using emoticons in my e-mails, because they convey my feelings.

—— **8.** Jin Hee always dresses too ornately. On the other hand her sister dresses too plainly.

—— **9.** The drought lasted twelve years; before the rains came back.

—— **10.** My neighbor's television was too loud. So I went over and asked her to lower the volume.

WRITING PROCESS WORKSHEET

Step 1: Analyzing the Assignment

Topic	Purpose	Source of Info	Length	Due Date	Presentation

Step 2: Brainstorming

put your
topic here

Step 3: Organizing Your Ideas

1. Thesis statement: _____

2. Are there any ideas from Step 2 that don't relate to your thesis statement? If so, cross them out.

3. Complete this outline for each body paragraph. Begin with the topic sentence (TS). You may need to increase or decrease the number of major supporting sentences (SS) and minor supporting sentences (ss). End with a concluding sentence (CS).

   TS _____

     SS _____

       ss _____

     SS _____

       ss _____

     SS _____

       ss _____

   CS _____

4. Fill in any gaps in support in the outline above by adding to the outline.

Step 4: Writing the First Draft

Write the first draft from your outline. Write the body paragraphs, the introductory paragraph, and the concluding paragraph. Put your paper aside for at least an hour before moving on to Step 5.

Step 5: Rewriting the First Draft

Check your paper in these areas. Mark any changes that you want to make.

Content: Are all the ideas relevant?

Is there adequate support?

Organization: Is your thesis statement at the end of your introductory paragraph?

Do you need topic sentences in your body paragraphs?

Is your concluding paragraph appropriate?

Vocabulary: Are your words too informal for academic writing?

Can you use a more descriptive word or a more accurate word?

Grammar: Are your sentences complete?

Are your verb tenses correct?

Are your nouns used correctly?

Are there any other grammar problems?

Mechanics: Have you used correct paragraph and essay format?

Have you used commas and semicolons correctly?

Step 6: Writing the Final (or Next) Draft

Write your final draft according to the revisions you made in Step 5.

Taking Essay Exams

Many of the tests you will take at your college or university will require an essay answer. These "essay answers" aren't necessarily organized like the essays you learned about in this book. An essay answer might be a five-sentence paragraph or several pages. The major difference between this type of writing and the paragraph and essay writing discussed in this book is, of course, time. You are expected to write these essay answers during class in a limited amount of time. With the pressure on, it is natural that you will not have as much control over grammar and punctuation as you do when you have a lot of time to write. However, you can follow some simple guidelines to help you maintain your overall organization and make your essay answers clear and understandable. Most instructors can overlook a few spelling and punctuation mistakes; after all, even native speakers make these kinds of errors sometimes. However, if your answer is difficult for your instructors to follow and understand, your grade will most likely be affected.

First, before you begin any test, look over the entire test and plan your time. Often, college and university tests have two types of questions: objective and subjective. Objective questions have answers that are either right or wrong and include question types such as true/false, multiple choice, and matching. Subjective questions require essay-type responses and are evaluated by your instructors. These question types include definition, short answer, and essay. Before you begin writing, note the point value given to each section of the test. This information will help you plan your test-taking time.

In general, it is a good idea to go through the objective questions rather quickly and save most of your time for the subjective questions. Some people prefer to answer the most difficult essay questions first to get them over with; others prefer to do the easier questions first to increase their confidence. Do whatever is best for you. However, leave some time at the end to reread your essay responses. Students often catch a lot of mistakes at this point because they can look at their writing more objectively.

In short, the most important point to remember is that it is usually *not* a good idea to take a test from beginning to end, starting when the professor says "go" and stopping when the professor says "time's up." Remember that everyone thinks differently and has a different path to success. Be sure to choose the path that works best for you.

Some Guidelines for Essay-Type Questions

- Some essay questions are not asked in question form. Instead, they start with an imperative verb that tells you to do something. Some common verbs used in essay-type questions and their meanings are listed here:

  1. Analyze: Separate a topic into smaller parts and explain each part.

  2. Compare and/or Contrast: Tell what is similar and/or different about two or more topics.

3. Define: Tell what a word or idea means.
4. Discuss: Give information about a topic.
5. Explain or describe: Tell how something works or what something is like.
6. Summarize: Tell the most important parts of a topic.
7. Synthesize: Put information from different sources together so that it is easy to understand.

- Answer the question in the first one or two sentences of your response. A instructor wants to know from the beginning that you are on the right track. Do *not* spend time writing an introductory paragraph. Remember that your time is limited. In addition, you don't have to get the reader's attention. Your instructor is already committed to reading your paper.
- Don't spend a lot of time writing a concluding paragraph. Just make sure you cover all your points in the main body of the essay.
- Organize your response in a coherent, cohesive fashion. Don't start writing without a plan in mind. Keep your organization simple. Use a basic type of organization, such as process, classification, persuasion, or comparison and contrast.
- Keep your response on target. Don't just write down everything you know about the topic. Often, this is a signal to instructors that you don't really understand the question and are hoping that the answer is somewhere in your response.
- Keep in mind that an important part of higher education in the United States is training students to synthesize and evaluate information. If you want to get a good grade, don't just repeat what the instructor has said in class or what you have read in a textbook. Instead, synthesize the two and add some observations of your own.

Writing Essays for Standardized Tests

Many of the standardized tests that are required for admission to a university or college, such as the TOEFL,® include essays. Often, you will have thirty minutes to answer this type of question. You may be asked to write about a social, political, or environmental issue, or an experience that you have had. You might also listen to part of a lecture, read a short passage, and then write a response that summarizes and compares and contrasts the information presented in each.

The main purpose of a writing sample on a standardized test is to show the *test giver* whether or not the *test taker* can communicate his or her opinions or synthesize and evaluate information in an organized, well-written way. Therefore, many of the guidelines that were discussed previously are also important to remember when taking this type of test.

Some Guidelines for Writing Essays on Standardized Tests

- You can usually find example questions and sample responses to common standardized tests on the test company's website. Read these examples to know what to expect and what is expected of you.
- Before you begin writing, think about what you are going to say. Some tests allow you to write notes on your own paper. Be absolutely sure that you are responding to what the test question is asking. As you are writing, stick to the point. Two of the most important criteria for evaluating this type of test are whether the writing is unified and whether it responds to all parts of the question.

- Before writing, think about an overall plan of organization. You can choose to write in a paragraph pattern (a topic sentence, supporting sentences, and a concluding sentence) or an essay pattern (an introductory paragraph with thesis statement, body paragraphs, and a concluding paragraph). The choice you make will probably depend on how much time you have, what the topic is, and how comfortable you feel writing in English. The key is to write a well-organized composition that has a short beginning, a well-supported middle, and (if time allows) a short end.

- Use your time effectively. Always bring a watch or clock with you, and check the time periodically. For a thirty-minute test, a good way to organize your time is:

  5 minutes: thinking and planning (organizing)
  20 minutes: writing
  5 minutes: rereading and checking for mistakes

- Take the time to reread what you have written. Even if you can spend only two or three minutes rereading, you may catch some grammar or spelling errors that can be easily corrected. Sometimes these simple errors can detract from your message and your grade.

Submitting handwritten assignments is no longer an option in most universities and colleges in the United States. It is expected that all papers will be typed on a computer. In fact, some professors ask students to submit their assignments by e-mail, eliminating the hard copy altogether. Below is a list of formatting guidelines. Following the list is a sample paper.

1. The margins should be set at an inch on all sides (top, bottom, right, and left).

2. The text is generally justified on the left, which means that each line comes out even at the left margin. Leave the right margin ragged—that is, not lined up evenly on the right side. Although this might not look neat to you, it makes your paper easier to read.

3. Use a common font, such as Times New Roman, Arial, or Georgia. Always use a 12-point font size. Don't use more than one font in your paper.

4. Your name, the course title, and the date should be placed in the upper right-hand corner. You may also include the professor's name below the course title. If you have more than one page, put your last name and the page number in the upper right-hand corner, beginning on the second page.

5. The title should be centered and spaced two lines below the date and two lines above the beginning of the paper. Use the word-processing program's centering icon to center the title.

6. Your paper should be double-spaced. It is not necessary to have an extra space between paragraphs.

7. The first line of each paragraph should be indented five spaces. The easiest way to do this is to use the TAB key.

8. The first letter of each sentence is capitalized. Leave one space between each word. There are no spaces between the last word and the period.

9. There are no spaces between a word and a comma, semicolon, or period. Leave one space after these punctuation marks.

10. In word-processing programs, sentences automatically continue onto the next line when there is not enough space for a word. Do not press "Enter" or "Return" at the end of a line unless, for example, you want to start a new paragraph.

11. Many word-processing programs automatically indicate when a word is misspelled. Some programs also check grammar. Although these tools are very helpful, be careful. Many will not highlight correctly spelled words that are incorrectly used. For example, if you type *to* when you mean *too*, your program may not indicate that it is wrong because *to* is a correctly spelled word. Therefore, no matter how much you trust your computer program, be sure to proofread your work.

Here is an example of a well-formatted academic paper.

Lydia Sanchez
English I
September 5, 2008

Small Things

Three of my experiences in the United States stand out in my memory as typically American. First of all, I remember coming down to breakfast at my host family's house on my first day there. My host mother had already left for work, her two children were eating some cereal, and their father was talking on the phone. He smiled at me and pointed to the refrigerator. I didn't understand, so I just smiled back. I went to school hungry that day. The second experience was trying to take a shower. I had no idea what the different knobs were for and struggled for about half an hour. Finally, I gave up and took a cold bath. The third incident occurred when I went to the supermarket. In my country, we always put our purchases in bags ourselves. When someone else started putting my groceries into a bag, I thought she was stealing my food, so I tried to hold on to it. When I finally realized what was going on, I was so embarrassed that I didn't think I could ever go into that store again. These three experiences showed me how cultural differences are often most obvious in minor, everyday events.

COMMON CONNECTORS

		Chronology	Description	Cause	Result	Unexpected Result	Contrast	Direct Contrast	Similarity
TRANSITIONS		first at first second third next after that at this point later on then at last finally	nearby to the left to the right		as a consequence as a result consequently therefore	however nevertheless nonetheless	however in contrast	however on the other hand	likewise similarly
CONJUNCTIONS	**SUBORDINATING**	after as before since until when while		as because since		although even though		whereas while	
	COORDINATING	and		for	so	but yet	but yet	but yet	both . . . and neither . . . nor not only . . . but also
PREPOSITIONS		after before since until prior to	above behind next to under on top of in front of	because of due to		despite in spite of	different from in contrast to	unlike	like similar to

COMMON CONNECTORS

	Addition	Example	Explanation	Emphasis	Condition	Most Important	Equal Importance	Conclusion
TRANSITIONS	furthermore in addition moreover	for example for instance	in other words that is	indeed in fact	in that case otherwise	above all most importantly most significantly most of all	for one thing for another thing equally important	all in all in conclusion in short in summary to sum up
CONJUNCTIONS COORDINATING	and							
CONJUNCTIONS SUBORDINATING								
PREPOSITIONS	in addition to							

The Paragraph Checklists and Peer Help Worksheets that appear throughout this book were designed to help you and your classmates look at your writing with a critical eye. Many of the checklists and worksheets in the book focus on one particular topic, but the worksheet below is more general and can be used to help you evaluate any academic essay.

CONTENT

1 What did you particularly like about this essay?

2 What is the rhetorical pattern used in this essay?

3 Do the individual paragraphs have unity? . . . . ❑
Point out to the writer any sentences you think are irrelevant.

ORGANIZATION

1 What kind of introductory paragraph does this essay have?
(Check one.)
   a. anecdote . . . . ❑
   b. historical introduction . . . . ❑
   c. general to specific . . . . ❑

2 Is there a strong thesis statement? . . . . ❑
If so, circle it. Underline the controlling idea. Put a box around the predictor, if there is one.

3 Do the body paragraphs have good coherence? . . . . ❑

4 What elements does the concluding paragraph have?
(Check all that apply.)
   a. summary . . . . ❑
   b. restatement of the thesis statement . . . . ❑
   c. final comment . . . . ❑

MECHANICS

1 Are capital letters, periods, commas, and semicolons used correctly? . . . . ❑
Put a question mark (?) by any punctuation you think is incorrect.

2 Are there any fragments, comma splices, or run-on sentences? . . . . ❑

If so, point them out to the writer.

PARAGRAPH AND ESSAY EVALUATION

There are many things to consider when evaluating academic writing. While different teachers and schools will use their own evaluation tools, most will include categories similar to those outlined in the form below.

Scoring		Aspects of Good Writing
		Content/Ideas
Very good:	25–23	
Good:	22–20	• has excellent support
Average:	19–17	• is interesting to read
Needs work:	16–0	• is unified
SCORE:		• follows the assignment

Organization

Scoring		**Paragraph**	**Essay**
Very good:	25–23		
Good:	22–20	• has topic sentence with clear controlling idea	• has introductory paragraph with clear thesis statement
Average:	19–17	• has supporting sentences	• has body paragraphs with good organization
Needs work:	16–0	• has concluding sentence	• has concluding paragraph
SCORE:		• has coherence and cohesion	• has coherence and cohesion

Grammar/Structure

Scoring		
Very good:	25–23	• demonstrates control of basic grammar (e.g., tenses, verb forms, noun forms, prepositions, articles)
Good:	22–20	
Average:	19–17	• shows sophistication of sentence structure with complex and compound sentences
Needs work:	16–0	
SCORE:		

Word Choice/Word Form

Scoring		
Very good:	15–14	• demonstrates sophisticated choice of vocabulary items
Good:	22–12	• has correct idiomatic use of vocabulary
Average:	11–10	• has correct word forms
Needs work:	9–0	
SCORE:		

Mechanics

Scoring		
Very good:	10	• has good paragraph or essay format
Good:	9–8	• demonstrates good control over use of capital letters, periods, commas, and semicolons
Average:	7–6	• demonstrates control over spelling
Needs work:	5–0	• doesn't have fragments, comma splices, or run-on sentences
SCORE:		

TOTAL SCORE:
(out of 100)

Comments

Below is a list of common correction symbols teachers use to correct or evaluate academic papers. Your instructor may use other symbols as well. Ask about any symbols you do not understand.

¶	Indent for paragraph.	
cap	Mistake in use of capital letter	(w)e went to (c)anada.
sp	Mistake in spelling	Don't (argu) with me.
p	Mistake in punctuation	You're late ○
c	Mistake in comma use	I left ○ but she stayed.
poss	Mistake in possessive	I washed (the) face.
wo	Wrong word order	He has a (shirt blue).
ww	Wrong word	The table is (tall).
wf	Wrong form of word	I enjoy (to ski).
ref	Unclear reference	Tom put (their) books away.
t	Mistake in verb tense	He (goes) yesterday.
prep	Mistake in preposition	He's married (with) her.
art	Add an article.	Jim ate ‸ banana.
agr	Mistake in verb agreement	Sue (know) how to dance.
#	Mistake in singular or plural	I have three (brother).
		I have one (sisters).
^	Add a word or words.	Six ‸ an even number.
X	Eliminate this word.	The ~~my~~ book is there.

frag	Fragment	*frag* ⟨At the restaurant.⟩
ro	Run-on sentence	*ro* ⟨Joe bought a new car it's a Honda.⟩
cs	Comma splice	*cs* ⟨I saw the cat, it was black.⟩
inf	Too informal for academic writing	*inf* The party was ⟨cool.⟩
?	Unclear	
OK	Teacher mistake. Ignore it.	

INDEX